Joyce

Blessings my sister!

The Last Three Tickets to Heaven

SANDRA THOMPSON WILLIAMS

Sandra J Williams
11/2018

*This book is dedicated to all those
generous enough to spread the good news
of the Gospel of Jesus Christ.*

Chapter One

"BUSTER, DON'T SWING SO HIGH!" Christina screamed at her eight-year-old son. "He's always trying to compete with the other boys," she explained to her neighbor, Rachel, as she monitored the children enjoying the park swings. "I think he's always trying to outdo Charlie! Cedric is the only one who is cool and calm about everything! If I go over there and supervise the pushing, Buster will say I'm treating him like a baby. Seems like every time I try to give him the benefit of using common sense, he just shows out in front of others," she explained.

"Good luck with that," Rachel said. "Remember the child is only eight."

"Don't say that around him or he'll correct you and say eight and a half," Christina said with a little giggle. "I really do enjoy these Saturday afternoons in the park," Christina said crossing her long legs as she sat on the park bench.

"I figure it's the least I can do for the kids," she said looking up at the sky.

"Especially since I don't have enough funds to take them to the amusement park very often."

"Quit putting that on the kids," Rachel said with a look of discerning knowledge while sitting beside her. It was one that her friend completely understood. "I heard you say last week that you were hoping for a tall, dark and handsome stranger to show up suddenly in this park."

"I said no such thing!" Christina argued while flipping her small, colorful beaded necklace with her right hand and placing the other on her attractive hip that complimented her small waistline. "I wouldn't be cheating on…"

1

"Oh save that for someone who doesn't know better," Rachel said. "Plus, I wouldn't call cheating on a cheater cheating!" she said emphatically.

"That's not fair," Christina exclaimed with her big brown eyes opening even larger than before.

"Well life's not fair either, and if your friend can't tell you the truth, who can?" Rachel blurted out quickly. Christina's five year old, Melissa, suddenly let out a sigh, picked up her jacks and ran to the swings.

"Speaking of life, here comes Mr. Marvelous now," Rachel said sarcastically.

A MAN MOVED WITH A BRISK WALK toward their bench. He had a slight limp and an angry look in his deep-set eyes. His backward cap seemed to give him a little height while it was obvious that it was there to cover his unkempt curly hair.

"Hi Marvin," Rachel said politely without any genuine feeling in her voice.

"Rache," Marvin answered with a nod while quickly turning his attention to Christina. "I need to see you for a minute," he said while grabbing her elbow with a little tug to get her from the bench. They walked about 10 feet toward the large oak and put their backs to Rachel. It didn't really disguise his purpose in coming to her. Rachel always knew when he showed up during the day it would be for one selfish reason. He needed money. She watched Christina attempt to walk away from Marvin. Then he said something that was inaudible to Rachel, but the impact of his words caused Christina to go back toward him. Christina reached into her knapsack hanging across her shoulder and pulled out some cash. She reluctantly gave it to him. He gave her a pseudo passionate kiss and walked quickly away.

RACHEL STOOD FROM THE BENCH to watch the children a little closer. She felt someone quickly grab her around the waist. She turned and saw it was Christina's baby girl. "Hey Lissa," she said to the child, "are you having fun?"

"Can I stay over with you tonight, Aunt Rachel?" she said with her deep dimples giving her the appearance of a cherub. "Can you ask Mommy if I can stay with you?" she pleaded.

"Why do you want to stay over with me?" Rachel asked sincerely. She thought Melissa's right dimple and the tiny mole over her right eye made her the cutest little five year old ever. "We're not doing anything in my apartment special this weekend," she insisted.

"I just do," Melissa expressed holding even tighter to her neighbor. She had known Rachel all her young life, and it felt like Rachel was a real aunt. She knew she had a real aunt in another city, but she hardly knew her mom's sister, Aunt Macey, who lived in Chicago. Even though they were only 100 miles apart, it seemed like a million miles in Melissa's mind.

Rachel was giving the notion some sincere thought. She was planning to do some deep cleaning this weekend. The landlord had done nothing about the roaches she reported seeing two weeks earlier. Although she was three floors down from Christina's apartment in their six-story building, they both said the little critters had shown up around the time that the newest tenants had moved in on the 6th floor, which was the top floor of the building. She had planned to get some industrial strength bug spray from her co-worker at the diner where she worked. She didn't really want to have Melissa in the way while she took care of this.

Christina started to head back in their direction. Rachel looked directly into the eyes of the sweet little child with her seemingly endless barrettes holding her short, stiff hair in place. Melissa must have sensed a negative response to her sincere request because it prompted two small tears to fall from her little round eyes.

"Well, I think that if you..." Rachel began.

3

HER VOICE WAS INTERRUPTED by the sound of music playing. She couldn't see the vehicle, but the Hurdy Gurdy circus tune always announced the coming of the neighborhood ice cream truck.

"Oh brother, here comes Stan the Ice Cream Man," Christina said with a long sigh. "And I don't have any more cash in my wallet."

"Oh, I got you covered," Rachel smiled. She wanted to laugh. Christina had a reputation for giving away her money to her live-in boyfriend. And she always said the same thing.

"I'll pay you back the next time I see you," Christina said. She could see the kids jumping from the swings as the sound of the approaching truck got louder. Half a dozen kids ran straight to the edge of the park to wait. However, their kids, Buster and Cedric and Charlie, raced to their mothers.

"Here comes The Three Musketeers," Christina said alerting Rachel.

"At this point, they're probably The Three Musty Teers," she said with a laugh.

THE CHILDREN WANTED TO BE FIRST IN LINE to try to pull for a prize when they got their cones, but that never happened. Some of the other kids always seemed to have their own money with them and didn't have to ask their moms. But this crew understood that things were harder in their households. They knew their moms worked as hard as they could to take good care of them. They didn't have a dad to depend on like some of their school friends. Christina's kids had two different dads. But neither would stick around when things were rough. The child welfare department wanted to go after them for child support, but Christina refused. She told the Social Service Administration that she didn't want retaliation or false hopes of getting a steady income from two undependable 'good for nothings'.

"Can I have a quarter, Mom? Please, please," Charlie asked, facing Rachel and nearly out of breath.

"Can I have 30 cents?" Buster said while extending his skinny,

4

dirty hand to Christina. "Aunt Rachel is treating everyone today," Christina said. Christina's kids shamefacedly turned toward Rachel and waited politely.

"Cedric, where are your glasses?" Rachel asked.

Cedric didn't answer. He just pulled them from his front pocket and put them on his face. He immediately noticed that Melissa's shoelaces were loose and tangled. He walked over to her and tied the laces neatly.

"Cedric, you've got a heart of gold. You're always so thoughtful of others," Christina said.

Cedric didn't say anything, but his chest stuck out proudly.

"Thanks, Cedric," Melissa said. She got closer to him and whispered in his ear, "Why are you winking at me?"

"I'm not winking," he said adjusting his glasses.

Rachel pulled out a dollar. "Why do you need an extra nickel?" she asked, staring at Buster. Although Buster was not her son, Rachel knew he sometimes got things confused because of his dyslexia. He worked really hard at trying to overcome the problem and the stigma that came with it. It mostly showed up when he was upset, nervous, or anxious. "I want to spin the wheel for a chance to win a prize," he said innocently.

"Like what?" Rachel asked.

"I saw a tattoo sticker in the prize box," he said with his eyes getting wider as he described the prize.

RACHEL WAS HARDLY PAYING ATTENTION. Her eyes had focused on Charlie's dirty fingernails and hands. Both sand and dirt had lodged beneath the nails. It was hard for her to imagine him eating ice cream with germs one step away from introducing them-selves to her child's intestinal system.

She was about to send him over to the water fountain or restroom, but it was on the other side of the park. Although she could see it from where she stood, she also saw strangers near it. She only recognized Daddy Long Legs. He was the gentleman who showed up in the park quite often to read his paper. He never bothered anyone. He would just smile and nod his head, and sometimes he'd whistle. Occasionally, he would pick up litter and make sure it was in the trash bin. No one knew his real name. They only knew he was extremely tall. No one knew or would admit knowing who nicknamed him Daddy Long legs. Christina said she heard a rumor that he was a retired basketball player.

Rachel rambled through her little purse and found an alcohol swab. She normally used them for removing her makeup when she wasn't home. When she found it, she cleaned Charlie's hands before he could think to object. Then she took her little green coin purse and emptied the contents in her hand. She retrieved two shiny dimes and gave both the dollar and dimes to Charlie.

"Get a scoop of ice cream for Melissa, Buster, and Cedric, and everybody gets to spin for a prize today."

Charlie took the money with a big smile and thanked his mother while beckoning for his brother and neighbors to follow his lead. Charlie ran ahead of everyone while Melissa skipped and tried to keep up with the gang. He arrived just after the first crowd of kids was leaving the truck. Charlie greeted Mr. Stan. He always parked his truck where it could be visible to all those enjoying the playground spot at the edge of the park's curb, which was across from the small flower garden considered a landmark for Cherry Blossom Park. Even without the noise of the truck's music, it would have been hard to miss the bright red letters painted on the truck. It read: 'Stan's Heavenly Ice Cream.'

"Hi, Mr. Stan!" Charlie greeted him.

"Hey, young man," he answered. "What can I do you for?"

The kids all laughed at his speech. They liked the funny way he spoke to them.

"I want strawberry," Melissa said, looking up at Charlie.

"I want chocolate," said Cedric, pushing the thick-lens glasses back up with his right pointer finger.

"Me too," Buster said.

"Well, I want vanilla, and everybody gets to spin," Charlie said sounding like the big man in charge.

"Oh, we're spinning today?" he asked rhetorically as he turned to the chest behind him to check the prize box. He made a grimace when he looked inside. There was only one prize left.

"Ladies first," he announced as he put the cone beneath the strawberry-marked opening in the machine.

He handed Melissa the cone then the hand-sized spinning wheel. Her arrow landed on five.

"Wow!" he said. "That means you pick something from this box." Melissa inserted her hand in the treasure box that he lowered from his window. Her small hand came out with a shiny purple ring that was all glass.

"Thanks, Mr. Stan," she said revealing a snaggle-tooth smile as she walked carefully back to show her mom and Aunt Rachel. She could have gone faster but didn't want to drop her ice cream.

MR. STAN COMPLETED THE OTHER THREE ORDERS and took the one dollar from Charlie. When Charlie tried to hand him the dimes, he held up his hand like a traffic cop.

"Well, boys, I got to tell you," he said, "I'm fresh out of prizes, but today is your lucky day." Buster licked his ice cream and challenged him on how it could be lucky if he was out of prizes.

"I've got something better," he said looking excited. He beckoned for Charlie to come closer so he could tell him something. He then whispered something in his ear that made Charlie look out toward his family and friends and then laugh. Stan the Ice Cream Man then reached beneath the cash register and pulled out an envelope. He bowed his head holding the contents near his heart. "Father, I pray that this special gift will make an eternal difference in the lives of many people. Let goodness and mercy follow the owners, in the name of Jesus Christ. Amen." He then passed the contents out to the boys.

"I was saving these for my own family," he said, "but I was just talking with my angel and he told me to give them to you boys."

"What is it?" Charlie asked with sincere curiosity.

"What is it?" Mr. Stan repeated with an inflection of surprise in his voice.

"Boys, you hold in your hands the last three tickets to heaven!" he exclaimed.

Buster looked at his friends and decided against laughing.

"Yes sir," Mr. Stan continued, "just read the instructions and one day your ride to heaven will show up and take you there in style," he said as he closed his window and prepared to drive away.

The boys shook their heads and headed back towards their mothers.

"I didn't want no stinking ticket," Charlie said throwing his ticket to the ground. "I wanted a tattoo."

"Young man, you dropped something," a voice said coming from behind them.

The shadowed figure seemed to loom over them like a towering building. It was Daddy Long Legs, and he had a stern look on his face.

Charlie quickly picked up the ticket, put it in his pocket and continued toward the bench where he left his mom and Christina.

THE CHILDREN WERE ENJOYING THE ICE CREAM so much that they quickly lost interest in the disappointment of not getting a prize. For the moment all seemed right with the world as they enjoyed their favorite flavor on that peaceful day in the park. They would remember this moment for a lifetime, but they didn't realize it quite yet. Their tongues were so engaged in licking the flavorful treat that they didn't see the large pickup truck speed right by them. Their attention was too focused on sweet perfection. In retrospect, the white pickup did seem to have a commercial ladder that protruded from the bed of the truck. The shiny steel caught the sunlight, and they did notice it from their peripheral view. But what happened next was incredible. The pickup failed to negotiate with the curb at the turnabout. The weight of whatever else was in that truck possibly caused the driver to lean heavily to the right. It was way to the right. So far that he could not possibly miss colliding with the ice cream truck where Stan the Ice Cream Man was starting to pull out.

THE SOUND WAS SO LOUD AND STARTLING that they all jumped and Cedric dropped his cone. That was nothing compared to what they were witnessing. The children's eyes increased to the size of a half dollar piece as they heard the catastrophic noise. A horrible collision had just taken place that left a ball of fire as red as blood, lighting up the sky just where the ice cream truck was parked. The crash caused both vehicles to be inflamed so much so that you could hardly distinguish one from the other. The boys ran close to their mothers to avoid sparks that were still flying. Christina had one hand over her mouth and the other hand extended to wrap the children around her. Rachel turned her children away from the scene so that they wouldn't go into shock.

Melissa began sobbing uncontrollably. Christina dropped to her knees to comfort her for what seemed like an eternity.

"Mr. Stan, Mr. Stan," Melissa said while shaking and trying to cover her eyes. "Help him, Mommy," she said weeping.

The next sound, in addition to the crackling of the consumed truck, was from someone shouting from the house across the street that they had just called for an ambulance and fire truck.

Convinced that there was nothing they could do, the young mothers quickly walked their children home, confused and dazed, with only the noise of the fire truck and gentle sobbing in the distant background.

Chapter Two

TWENTY YEARS LATER

The last call for Flight 675 was announced between an orchestra's rendition of "It's the Most Wonderful Time of the Year" and "Frosty the Snowman." Graciela boarded the plane hopeful that she'd have room to stretch out and read without having to share her space too closely with anyone. She overheard an airline worker say there were at least 350 people on the flight. She knew more people would be traveling for the holiday, but that wouldn't fill a 747, she reasoned within herself. She took the earliest flight available because most people did not like to travel in the wee hours of the morning. At least that's what she convinced herself. When she selected her row on yesterday, no one else had claimed the seat beside her. She was hopeful that nothing had changed.

Somewhere in the line behind her, someone was playing Sinatra's version of "Silent Night." She hoped the song was a prediction for her long flight. She could use the sleep. She flipped open her phone case so the attendant could scan her boarding ticket. It was easy, since she only had the one carry-on item. She finally made her way down the long corridor and exchanged pleasant good mornings with three of the five flight attendants. It was a large plane, but thankfully the aisles were wide enough to easily find her seat.

There it was just ahead of her, seat 28C. Her assigned seat was next to the window. A middle-aged man of about 60 years old sat in the aisle seat. No one was in the middle seat, and only a few people were left to board behind her. There were quite a number of empty seats in the back rows. Graciela put her luggage in the overhead compartment and slammed the door shut. The noise nearly frightened the half sleepy passengers within earshot. The gentleman passenger on her row stood up and stepped aside so she could slide into her seat. He then chose another seat behind her. It seemed obvious to her that he didn't want his original assigned seat and was fishing for an empty aisle seat to substitute. This may be a nice flight after all, she thought to herself.

Graciela put her purse on the floor beneath the seat directly in front of her. She made sure that she removed her neck pillow first, then fastened her seatbelt and pulled the shade down at her window. She figured she could make up for the sleep she had lost in another 60 seconds or so. She gently let her head rest toward the window and slowly tuned out what was around her as she started to drift.

"HEY, HEY, HEY!" someone shouted from the far end of the plane. "Good morning, world!" soon followed and other loud greetings along with laughter as a group of men interrupted the tranquil plane and headed for the back. Some appeared unsteady while grasping seat after seat on the way to their row. Graciela smelled a distinct odor of alcohol as they passed. She knew it was too early for most people to drink and decided that this group had never gone to bed.

Oh no, she thought. Early morning ramblers.

The group of four guys passed her and went two rows beyond. Thank goodness, she thought as she adjusted her body in the seat and turned again slowly toward the window. Then three people of Asian descent followed the rowdy crowd and sat across from her. She was still safe and kept her hopes alive that no one else would come.

"Where's Mark?" someone shouted. "Did we lose Mark?" There was more laughter, and suddenly one final passenger headed down the aisle reading the numbers as he moved closer and closer to the back.

"Oh, there he is!" one of them said rather loudly.

He smiled and waved at his buddies and stopped at Graciela's row. "There's the groom," one of them shouted and again broke into ridiculous laughter. He in turn saluted them and put his carry-on item in the overhead compartment.

"Hello," he said to Graciela as he tried to get comfortable in the aisle seat where he could glance back at his buddies. As soon as he opened his mouth, she detected alcohol again and wanted to get to sleep as soon as possible. "Morning," she answered in her 'I don't want to be bothered' voice as she tilted her head and faced the window.

"I guess it is morning," he said. "But I haven't been to bed yet," he explained with a little laugh. "Too busy celebrating," he continued. Graciela smiled and wished he would take the hint that she wasn't interested in his story. He, of course, continued as most intoxicated people do and wanted to spill his life story line by line by line.

She tried to close her eyes and ignore him, but he touched her arm when she wasn't paying attention. She thought that was rude, but explaining to a functioning intoxicated person that they are being inappropriate gets you nowhere. She knew that from growing up.

THE INTERCOM INTERRUPTED his rambling sentences as the captain welcomed everyone aboard. Next the stewardess explained the emergency evacuation plan and welcomed everyone again.

"Did I tell you that my name is Mark?" he asked.

"Nice to meet you," Graciela said.

"Well, what's your name?" he insisted louder than she would have anticipated. "I'm Graciela," she said, "but everyone calls me Grace."

He turned and looked toward his buddies and said, "Hey guys, this is Grace."

They were starting to drift off and didn't respond to his introduction. "That's my posse," he said with admiration.

"Nice," Graciela said.

"Are you married, Grace?" he asked sincerely.

"Engaged," Graciela answered.

"Me too! Well, where's the lucky guy?" he said looking around at men in seats in close proximity to their seats.

"He's waiting for me to get home," she said trying not to give too much information to this complete stranger.

"Home, home on the range," he sang out. "I'll be home for Christmas," he concluded. Thankfully, for Graciela's sake, people seemed to completely ignore his singing. "So, where's home?" he almost whispered, starting to realize that his voice was carrying further than he intended. "We're headed to New York. Is that where you live?" he asked pointedly.

Graciela nodded and smiled. She appreciated that he finally understood that he was louder than necessary.

"How'd you meet?" he said in a chummy tone, usually reserved for best friends. He adjusted his seat slightly. He tried to move it back, but the man behind him was rather tall and there wasn't much space to get comfortable.

She saw there was no way out of this ambush conversation and decided to talk freely with Mark. After all, she reasoned within herself, I'll never see him again.

"We met in an elevator," she began.

"Were you going up or was he going down, down, down?" he asked.

Graciela ignored the question and just stared at him.

"Well, were you going somewhere or just playing on the elevator?" he asked.

"Well, it, well I was actually on the elevator by myself at first," she admitted.

"I had just left the hospital cafeteria to return to my shift on the sixth floor. It had been a horrible day," she said wringing her slender hands. "One of my patients had coded and was revived twice before we found out they were on a DNR—that's a do not resuscitate order," she explained.

"I know," he said, almost appearing to be sobering up.

"Well the elevator had recently been serviced about a week earlier," she continued. "I thought the light was a little dim when I stepped inside, but I got in anyway. I hit the button for my floor and

13

it moved swiftly then came to a sudden halt with a jerk. My world went dark. I thought I was going to faint because I could smell something like burnt rope or rubber."

"Then what happened?" Mark asked.

"I thought about my nursing training and told myself to calm down and use the emergency phone," she explained. "Well, I picked up the phone and got the emergency service," she said. "They asked me if anyone was with me and I told them I was alone. They said someone was on the way and to just remain calm. But when she said that to me, the elevator moved suddenly and then there was a jolt. I actually fell to the floor sobbing. I don't know how long I cried. The elevator was actually between floors.

"So a fireman removed the top of the elevator ceiling and came inside of it with me. I think he went through a crawl space to get to it. He had a flashlight and tried to reassure me. I kept saying that I was going to die. I was hysterical. He told me not to say it, but I couldn't help it. I told him it was Friday the thirteenth and I was going to die.

"He whispered in my ear. And what he said calmed me down. Then he told me that if we did die, he knew where he was going. That sort of shocked me and got my full attention. I asked him what he meant by that. He said he had a ticket to heaven. That really made me mad and curious at the same time. He said he carries it with him all the time. He reached into his fireman outfit and pulled out a card and read it to me."

Graciela paused at that moment and took a breath.

"Well, what did it say?" Mark asked anxiously. "Don't keep me in suspense!"

Graciela reached into her handbag and pulled out a wallet. Inside a small side zipped pocket was a laminated card. She retrieved it and put away the wallet.

"Dear friend," she began reading. "Today I have good news. If you believe the words on this card, you can take a trip to heaven and

14

meet me. My name is Jesus. I am God's only son. I died for you so that you can come back to heaven with me and meet my father. I have watched you all your life, and I want you to know that I love you with an everlasting love. This ticket only works if you turn it over and repeat the words. They are only effective if you believe them."

Graciela turned the card over and continued reading. "Dear Jesus. Come into my heart and save me from my sins. I acknowledge that I need you as my Savior. I love you and I will follow you for the rest of my life. I ask this in your precious name. Amen. Dear friend, if you meant what you just prayed, keep this ticket close to you. It is now stamped for heaven and someday I will bring you with me into my kingdom."

Graciela looked up smiling and was met with a sour face. "Do you mean to tell me you fell for that?" Mark asked with a shocked expression.

"It worked for me," she said. "I calmed down and he let me have the card. Twenty minutes later, we were out of the elevator and I felt like a totally different person."

"I don't believe in anything I can't see," Mark blurted.

"That's not true," Graciela said. "You take continuous breaths and you don't pause to examine the air that you can't see!" she said.

"That's different," he said, rubbing his hands through the locks of his hair. It was apparent that he was getting sleepy. The alcohol was wearing him down.

"You can't see your brain or your heart, but you believe you have one," she said.

"Well, something's wrong with my brain, cause I make stupid decisions, and the only reason I know I have a heart is because it's been broken so many times," he said.

"I called on Jesus once as a child and he didn't help me," he said angrily. "If he was real, bad things wouldn't have happened to me. I saw then I would have to fight for myself the rest of my life. I was raised in an orphanage after my parents died," he admitted. "It was not a kind place. Sometimes we were abused and sometimes we were taken advantage of," he said. "But that's another story. Anyway, I don't believe in Jesus or any ticket to heaven."

Graciela was surprised at his response to her true story. After all, he asked for the information.

"Bad things happen to everyone," Graciela confessed. "This is a fallen world," she continued. "That's why I'm preparing to leave it by using my ticket to heaven," she concluded.

"Would you like a soft drink or pretzel?" the attendant interrupted.

"I'd like something just a little stronger," he said.

"I'd like a Coke," Graciela said. The attendant conversed with Mark about available alcoholic beverages. Graciela adjusted her neck pillow and made herself comfortable in the seat.

FOR A FEW MINUTES, THERE WAS SILENCE between her and Mark. Thankfully, the attendant returned with their beverages. Grace indirectly watched as Mark fumbled through his wallet and finally found his credit card.

"Let's toast to our fiancés," Mark suggested after paying for his drink.

Graciela was willing to do about anything to help shut him up. "Here's to our fiancés," Graciela said, raising her clear plastic cup filled nearly to the brim. His cup touched hers.

"Well," he said, "to-ooo?"

She finally caught on and filled in the blank with, "To Bernard, or Buster is what everybody calls him," she said smiling.

"To Buster," he repeated.

"What's your fiancé's name?" Graciela asked.

"Brian," he said.

Chapter Three

GENERAL GALSTER STARED OUT the second floor window of the officer's quarters. The two hour meeting earlier with his staff was very unsettling. He had to put up a convincing argument. He could remember the day when his advice went unquestioned. These days, he told himself, congressional whipper snappers are all into military business. He couldn't even drop a bomb without notifying Washington. Yet he knew what he had to do. He gathered his jacket and hat and headed for the office.

The evening sun would soon be setting on this foreign land he had to call his home base for the past 36 months.

Army life was predictable at times and very unpredictable at others. He had served more than 35 years and made his way up the ranks. He took pleasure in giving young soldiers a hard time. The army was no nursery. Weaklings should take their bleeding hearts and join the Red Cross. The discipline of a soldier was necessary. Winning a battle depended on it. He earned every star and stripe he was ever awarded. His great-grandfather had died serving in the Civil War. The Confederates may have lost the battle, but he swore to his father that he would make their family name great again. Now here was his chance. He had to convince a soldier that he had a fifty percent chance of survival, even if all the data proved otherwise. He wasn't about to tell him there was only a ten percent chance. Statistics prove that if a man thinks he can survive, he will. He would leave it at that.

He knew it would be a miracle if half the men survived the mission. But he knew it would be a feather in his cap if the mission were accomplished. In addition to this, the higher he ascended, the better his retirement amount would be. He wasn't satisfied being a brigadier general. He wanted to retire as a lieutenant general, major general or higher.

His reputation for being tough was well earned. He came up the hard way, and so would every soldier under his leadership. He prided himself on taking snotty nosed kids and turning them into men. The army didn't need any mama's boys. He hated it had taken so long to convince his superiors that this mission was the right thing to do. After all, he recalled saying to them before resting his case, this country was built on making hard decisions that threatened the lives of the men. Wasn't our country worth it?

He had to smile within himself for building such a remarkable case. Deep down he didn't really care if the men survived or not; he had a war to win. It wasn't going to be won if he had to consider every single life, every single day before making the plans to conquer enemy territory. There was one soldier that he was never really able to whip in shape. He was a know-it-all and a card carrying Christian. A lifelong atheist, General Galster didn't approve of Christians who had to pray about everything. He just wanted them to make up their own minds. That's what he had done all his life.

GENERAL GALSTER KEPT WALKING until he entered the meeting hall. Strategies were unfolded in this room. He slowly opened the conference room door. He could see Charlie sitting in the second row.

"Attention!" said the Lieutenant Colonel who stood just inside the door. Charlie jumped to attention and saluted the General.

In his heart the General felt Charlie was perfect for the job because he was expendable. He had caused the soldiers to be a little too soft. He had caught him on several occasions appearing to be proselytizing. There was no room for that in the army. Men needed to be tough, strong and daring without depending on what they considered to be a Supreme Being, he thought. He felt he was Supreme enough.

"At ease, Captain," the General said in his authoritative tone. He then nodded for the Lieutenant Colonel to leave. The General pulled out a chair and sat directly in front of Charlie. "I've got a proposition for you, Captain. I'll be frank in saying it's a sensitive situation but includes a great opportunity."

"Yes sir," Charlie responded. He wasn't fond of the General, but he did respect him. He had to. They had bumped heads a few times, but Charlie was able to overcome through prayer. He had actually obtained the respect of his fellow troopers for being such a great and successful Captain in nearly all of his feats. It was no secret to anyone on the base that he was always competitive in his missions.

"The army needs to get a small brigade behind a classified post," the General began. "It won't be a cakewalk, and there's some information that we can't seem to acquire any other way. Now there's a fifty percent chance that the squad may be captured," he lied. "These are radical extremists, and well you know what we have had to deal with this last year. We can only send volunteers. It's common knowledge that you've got great influence in your squad."

Charlie liked the sound of this mission. He had been beating the odds his whole time in the service. He had a hard time paying attention because he was imagining himself a hero. He would certainly be handsomely rewarded with a promotion. He was sure of that. Now, the part about influencing his fellow soldiers bothered him. Even though they referred to him as 'Commando' when playing around, he knew that the soldiers that he called his pals truly did respect him. But would they respect him enough for a fifty percent chance of getting captured? That was the question. Charlie was aware of all the talk that servicemen make regarding volunteering. Volunteering is like jumping off a cliff," he was told, "and no cliff is a good cliff no matter how wonderful the view may be."

The General continued to talk to him about what a valiant role he would be playing. But Charlie's mind was ten years in the past at his high school graduation. Senior superlatives were being announced. His good friend Buster was named the most compassionate senior. Charlie was named the most likely to succeed. He was proud of that honor. He didn't know why he was driven to do better than others, but he was.

He was willing to accept harm to his body if it meant the greater good and some true recognition.

"Can I have a day to think about it, General?" he asked.

"Soldier, take all the time you need," he responded as he stood. "Just let me know by tomorrow," he said without smiling.

Charlie jumped to his feet. "One day should be enough, sir," he said as he saluted the General.

"I'm sure whatever decision you make will be the right one," General Galster said as he left the room. It felt good to get back in the fresh air. The heavy guilt a normal commander would have felt was nowhere near the radar of this hard-nosed General. He felt nothing. Yet he knew in time he would justify his actions. He always did. It was for the good of the entire country that he made these weighty decisions.

Charlie grabbed the chair and put it back in place. He stood looking at the photographs hanging on the wall. Pictures of all the important leaders were there. He could not help but imagine that someday his picture could be among the celebrated military leaders. He would be the person young soldiers would have to salute and obey.

CHARLIE LOOKED AT HIS WATCH. It was 1400 hours. Good, he was sure he could catch his friend. No matter how anxious he was for a mission, he would take time to meet with his buddy. Lunch was over by now, so he headed straight for his office.

He wasn't sure what he was feeling. He just believed that this mission must be awfully serious for him to have a special audience with the General himself. He approached his friend's office and stopped at the receptionist's desk.

20

He saluted the receptionist. It made him a little uncomfortable being outranked by a woman younger than himself. But he couldn't help but salute and smile at the same time. He thought she was very pretty. They had one date together, but it was a double date. Since then, they would sometimes eat in the mess hall. He was smitten but was trying to take it slowly. He would sometimes daydream about her and even dream about her. She came from a military family. It was kind of hard to impress her. Plus he felt he needed to convince this military brat that there was only one God. When they had the discussion once, it didn't seem to matter to her which one he served. That bothered him tremendously.

"At ease, Captain," said Major Butler.

"Hello, Bonnie," Charlie said trying to keep his voice low enough that no one else could hear but the Major. "I was just thinking," he said. "I bet some of your friends called you BB when you were growing up. Not because you're Bonnie Butler but because you're Bonnie Beautiful," he said with a wink.

Major Butler tried to no avail to keep a straight face, but she blushed and said, "How can I help you, Captain Grimes?"

"I'd like to see Chaplain Bartley," he said with a serious face.

"I don't believe you have an appointment, Captain," she said looking through her scheduling calendar.

"You're right," he admitted. "I don't, but it is of major urgency that I speak with him," he continued while using his eyes to stare at the door behind her. It was as if he willed it to open. Then it did.

Charlie quickly stood at attention while he saluted Chaplain Bartley.

"At ease, Captain," the Chaplain said. "Are you here to see me or my assistant?" he asked half-jokingly.

"You, sir," Charlie answered with a laugh.

"Come on in," he said. "We haven't chatted for a while."

CHARLIE ANXIOUSLY FOLLOWED the Chaplain back into his office. He had been there many times when he was first deployed to that location. He was new to combat and needed answers that he believed only a man of God could give.

Most of his previous assignments were for peacekeeping, but he had also been involved in some military activity where several soldiers had lost their lives through dangerous training. Things had calmed a bit, but those first months in the desert land were very hard on him.

He found it comforting to see the crucifix on the wall and the sign on the Chaplain's desk that said "Peace to all" in ten different languages. He noticed the Hanukkah and Christmas cards that were lined up on the side of the desk.

"Pull up a chair, Captain," the Chaplain said gesturing toward one of three chairs positioned against the wall. "We haven't had a good chat for a few months. What's on your mind?"

"Well," Charlie began, "I need to make a big decision."

"Is it military or personal?" the Chaplain asked. "You do understand that I can't make any military decisions for you, don't you, Captain?" the Chaplain asked directly, leaning forward on the desk.

"Oh, I understand that," Charlie said nodding his head. "I'm looking for a, well … maybe, perhaps a sign," Charlie finally confessed.

"From God?" the Chaplain asked looking directly into Charlie's puzzled looking face. "I've never asked you this, but have you confessed Jesus as your Savior?

"Yes, sir," Charlie confessed. "I followed the instructions of a minister at a youth camp many years ago, and I meant every word I said."

"Good for you, soldier," the Chaplain said smiling. "Have you been reading the Bible since then?"

"Honestly, sir, I haven't been as faithful to reading it as I should have been," he answered. "There's a lot I just don't understand," he said dropping his head for a moment.

"Do you mean about life, the war or the Bible?" the Chaplain questioned.

Charlie leaned in with a serious expression and said, "All of the above."

With that statement, the Chaplain put a large smile on his face and began a chuckle that grew into a large belly laugh. It was loud and somewhat out of order in Charlie's mind. But the sincerity and genuineness were contagious. He wasn't sure why it happened, but he also began to laugh. He laughed until a small tear released itself from his eye.

The Chaplain handed him a regulation box of tissue and both began to compose themselves.

"Chaplain, why are we laughing?" Charlie asked sincerely.

"It's the medicine of the soul, Captain," the Chaplain answered. He then reached for his Bible and began thumbing through it to find a certain passage.
"HERE IT IS. PROVERBS 17:22," he pointed out.

> "A merry heart does good, like medicine But a broken spirit dries the bones."

He flipped through a few more pages.

"I also want to read you Proverbs 3:5," he said, suddenly turning serious

> "Trust in the Lord with all thine heart; and lean not unto thine own understanding. 6 In all thy ways acknowledge him, and he shall direct thy paths."

He closed the book with a small thud that seemed to echo throughout the room. "I understand that you want answers," he began. "I certainly don't have all the answers to life's problems, whether they are about war, peace or other issues regarding life. But I have learned to trust in God and to allow him to speak to me any way he desires. Look, soldier, if I had all the answers, I wouldn't have chaplain over the door. Instead it would say Almighty God," he said with a chuckle.

"I hear you," Charlie said. "It's just that my decision involves more people. If it was just me, it wouldn't be as difficult," he said.

The Chaplain sat back in his chair and looked up at the ceiling. "Looks like you need to have a heart-to-heart talk with your father about this."

Charlie looked confused about what the Chaplain was saying. "With all due respect, sir, I don't remember my father," Charlie said. "He died years ago."

The Chaplain seemed to ignore Charlie as he unlocked the bottom drawer of his desk. He reached in and pulled out a book that was worn but intact. He handed the book to Charlie, who read the title out loud.

"My Utmost for His Highest," Charlie read aloud. "Oh, sir. I apologize. I thought you meant, well, never mind."

"I want you to read this book," the Chaplain instructed. "Get to know more about your Heavenly Father," he said in a father's tone of voice."He's been waiting."

With that last piece of advice, Charlie stood, thanked the Chaplain and gave his dismissal salute.

Chapter Four

MARK WAITED FOR A REACTION from Graciela. There were no words that followed. He took her non-reaction as a negative vibe. Her brief silence made him assume she was homophobic.

Graciela didn't know what to say. She couldn't congratulate him because that would be dishonest. She always felt marriage was between a man and a woman. She didn't want to say anything that would be taken as negative because he might feel she was judging him. So she said nothing.

"Well?" Mark said as if he were waiting on an answer to a question.

"Yes, Mark?" Graciela said turning away from the window and toward him.

"How do you feel about my fiancé being a man?" he said.

"Does it really matter?" she said. She was sure he assumed she was uncomfortable talking to him. He probably thought she was self-righteous, and she knew that she wasn't.

"Humor me," he said with a yawn. Graciela took that gesture as a tell-tale sign that he was getting sleepy. She was hopeful because she didn't want to have this conversation. It was hard to win when people were looking for opposition.

"Tell me what you really think," he encouraged as if they were old friends. She assumed the alcohol had warmed him up.

She gently let her head fall back on the headrest of her chair. Then she put her remaining soda on her tray.

"Can I take that?" the flight attendant asked suddenly interrupting her thoughts. Graciela handed the soda to the attendant and exhaled. "I feel sorry for you," she said. "I think you are looking for love and acceptance in a very dark place."

"What? You feel... Why?" he asked emphatically as if it was absurd to feel that way. "I'm successful, I've overcome many odds and I have a fright buture," he managed to get out with a slur.

"A bright future," Graciela corrected while turning her head away to smile at his stutter. But when she turned towards him again, he was asleep.

Just like a baby, she thought. Put up a big fuss then fall asleep.

GRACIELA'S MIND WENT BACK THREE YEARS. A small tear escaped her left eye before she could catch it. She remembered her cousin's final days in the hospital. The visit was bittersweet. He refused visitors from everyone except her. When she visited, she made sure it was a time that she was not on duty. She didn't want any problems associated with being there to hold her cousin Vincent's hand. He deserved that.

Vincent was a strong-willed child. He was the cousin everyone wanted to hang out with. He was daring and so sure of himself. He could get nearly any kid to follow in his footsteps. He was on the path to being a great leader.

He wasn't perfect, but he wasn't nearly the bully his teachers had later made him out to be. They just kept labeling him. They even convinced his parents that he was on the road to no good.

Graciela was always the teen to take up for her cousin. She knew him better than most. She knew he had a good heart. She had witnessed him helping his elderly neighbor cut the grass, and he was the one who threatened the neighborhood bully so the other kids could hang on to their lunch money.

HOW LIFE WOULD HAVE TURNED OUT DIFFERENTLY if it wasn't for one strange weekend. Her reminiscing took her back ten years. She was preparing to complete her senior year. Vincent was short two credits and was taking makeup classes in the evening. One night there was a fight. Vincent wasn't in the fight but tried to break it up. The police were called, and they took the troublemakers and Vincent to the night jail at the juvenile center. He was labeled an instigator by the teacher. The fact that the teacher was out of the classroom when the fight started didn't carry enough weight to excuse him.

That same weekend, Vincent's parents were out of town at a funeral. He had no one to pick him up from jail that night. He was too embarrassed to call her parents. When his parents finally got the call, he had spent two days in jail. The bailiff admitted that there was a mix up with the paperwork. He should never have been left overnight in the jail. The other students were all released. But it was too late when they came to get him. Vincent had been raped in the minimum security facility. The local city jail was full due to a local protest. The judge ordered that 10 men be taken to the juvenile facility temporarily. They were never supposed to be left there overnight.

Vincent was never the same. Everyone saw the change in his personality, but no one could explain it. His shame brought a lasting scar on his life and he was never able to overcome it. He went from an outgoing young man to a withdrawn young adult to a promiscuous outsider. He was not allowed back in school to complete his senior year. With no real intervention, he ended up back in a real jail doing some real time for theft. Two years after his release, he was nearly unrecognizable. Unable to afford a hired attorney, his parents relied on a public defender. His defense was virtually worthless.

MISUNDERSTOOD AND SHUNNED by most of his family and childhood friends, he ended up on the south side of town. It was deemed the seedy part of the city. His neighborhood was known for harboring societal rejects like drug addicts, prostitutes and released offenders. Everyone knew he had become a part of the homosexual community.

The news of Vincent's whereabouts sometimes found its way to

Graciela while attending nursing school. Part of her studies took her to the wards where there were societal rejects dealing with deadly diseases. That's where she found her dear cousin, and that's where she prayed her first real prayer. She asked God to please take him so he wouldn't continue to suffer the miserable pain he was enduring. She was never sure if God heard her. But her cousin did die a short time later.

Since that time, of course, thanks to her fiancé, she had a real relationship with God. She was still learning about the God of the Bible. But she knew enough to understand what breaks his heart. Unable to resist any longer, she gently laid her right hand on Mark's arm and said a quiet prayer. In an inexplicable way, when she touched him and prayed, she felt rejection and abuse. Tears clouded her view. Somehow she knew these were feelings he had lived with most of his life. She prayed for Mark and every boy who had his innocence stolen on his journey to manhood. She prayed that the grace of God would interfere with their life and introduce them to wholeness again.

Chapter Five

"NEXT IN LINE," the teller said trying to get the attention of the young woman looking around.

The young lady stepped to the teller's window and plopped down a deposit slip and a wad of cash. It was two hundred dollars. There was a fifty dollar bill on top and one hundred and fifty singles.

The teller took the deposit slip and flipped it over.

"I'm sorry, miss," he said. "I need your account number to deposit this," he said nicely.

The young lady looked a little confused.

"Oh, I need to open a new account," she said shyly. "I used to have an account here, but it's probably closed cause that was a long time ago," she continued. The blank stare of the clerk made her feel embarrassed and she held her head slightly down. "Can I do it now?"

"Actually, miss, you need to see a bank representative," he said. "If you'll have a seat over there," he said pointing to the right, "someone will be with you shortly."

She nodded her head with gratitude and followed his instructions.

TWO MINUTES LATER, a young man in a dark blue suit approached her.

"Ma'am, I can see you next," the gentleman said. "Just follow me."

He walked to an office with a broad window and glass door.

He gestured for her to have a seat as he sat down behind the brown oak desk. "How can I help you?"

"I need to open a bank account," she said. She looked around as if she were afraid that someone would hear her.

"Sure, we can take care of that," he said. He pulled a form from the drawer and asked for her name. She looked up anxiously at the clock in his office.

"Melissa Miller," she said.

"Address?" he continued.

"5241 32nd Street," she said.

Suddenly he stopped writing and looked directly into her face. He seemed to concentrate on the deep dimples in her cheeks.

"Lissa?" he said.

Melissa stared back into his face. She knew there must be a connection. No one called her Lissa except those from her old neighborhood.

"Who are you?" she said cautiously.

"I'm Cedric," he said. "Cedric Grimes, Rachel's son."

Melissa's eyes grew large and her dimpled smile revealed a beautiful set of teeth.

"I didn't recognize you without your glasses," she said.

"I have contact lenses now," he said smiling. "How have you been?" he asked in a sincere tone.

Then as suddenly as her smile had appeared, it disappeared. She dropped her head and said, "Ok."

"What do you mean ok?" he said. "You look great. You're just a lot skinnier than when you were a teenager. I don't think I've seen you in what…"

"About 12 years," Melissa offered. "It was my mom's wedding," she said.

"Yeah, I was so sorry to hear about her passing so soon after the wedding. What was it?" Cedric asked.

"Cancer," Melissa answered. "It was in the final stage when it was detected," she said with a small hint of emotion.

"Where did you and Buster go after that?" he asked. "My mom said she lost touch with you after the marriage."

"We went to live with my aunt in Chicago," she said. "It wasn't the best life, but we had a roof over our heads. Buster left home as

30

soon as he turned eighteen."

Cedric looked at his watch and back at Melissa. "Do you want to go to lunch?" he asked. "I mean, when we finish this business. You can leave your car here."

"I took a cab here," she said. "My car is not working now."

"Perfect," he said. "We can have lunch and I can take you home or wherever you need to go."

Cedric completed his questions and opened the account for Melissa. She said she had more to deposit.

Melissa's eyes widened with excitement. "Do you really want to?" she asked.

"I'd love to," he answered. "Wait here for a moment," he requested.

HE LEFT THE ROOM AND SPOKE TO A CO-WORKER before returning to Melissa.

"I know several restaurants that are real close," he said while waiting for Melissa to follow him.

Melissa said nothing but marveled at how her childhood friend had turned into a real gentleman. He led her to a modern sedan that was clean and showed the pride of ownership.

"What kind of food do you enjoy?" he asked while closing her door as she slid into the leather seat.

"I'm not really picky," she answered when he was behind the wheel. "I can eat a burger nearly every day," she said laughing.

He started the quiet engine and pulled onto a parking lot in about seven minutes.

"It's not fancy, but the food is on point," he said.

THEY WALKED INTO THE RESTAURANT beneath an awning that read 'Tony's Hot Grill.' Melissa noticed right away that the decor was very seventies in design.

"Do you like the retro look?" Cedric asked.

"It's definitely different," she said, observing the jukebox and pictures of old singers framed everywhere.

"It kind of reminds me of...."

"Our childhood?" he said cutting her off.

"I think so," Melissa answered with her eyes wandering around the simple restaurant.

The place was only half full in spite of the noon hour.

"How much time do you get for lunch? Will you have enough time to eat? Where is the waiter?" Melissa seemed to blurt out unexpectedly.

"One hour, yes, and I don't know," Cedric answered.

Melissa was embarrassed by her own words. "I'm sorry, I didn't mean to act like a mother hen," she said.

"It's ok. I appreciate your concern," Cedric added.

"I'll try to pick something simple," Melissa said.

"That won't be difficult," he said passing her the menu that was beneath the ketchup.

She took one look at the menu after opening it, then looked into Cedric's face.

They both broke into laughter. There were only two items on the menu. It featured burgers five ways. There were turkey, beef, chicken, veggie and tofu burgers. Then there was salad five ways. It offered potato salad, green salad, pasta salad, bean salad and fruit salad.

"You said you could always eat a burger," he said smiling. "At this restaurant, you will always have a burger."

Melissa let her light jacket slip from her shoulders. Laughter had allowed her to warm up quickly. Although it was one of the mildest Decembers on record for that city, she cautiously wore a jacket just in case the weather changed, since she often rode public transportation.

With the jacket completely off, she turned slightly to hang it on her chair back. That's when Cedric noticed her arm. Her sleeve was slightly out of place and exposed a surprising mark. She had a tattoo that Cedric had only seen once before, but he never forgot its meaning.

DURING HIS COLLEGE STUDIES, he took a class on social behavior that included cults, social trends and the tattoo nation. He noticed that Melissa's tattoo was a faceless person with a tear drop. When she turned back around, she quickly straightened her sleeve. Just then a waiter appeared.

"Welcome to Tony's," a waitress said, pulling the pencil from her carefree updo hairstyle. "What can I get you folks?" she asked hurriedly.

Cedric nodded at Melissa. "Oh, I'll have the beef burger, medium well with just lettuce," she said.

"And your side?" the waitress asked never looking up from her paper.

"Green salad with French dressing," Melissa said completing her order.

"Oh, I'll take a Coke," she added.

"And you, sir?" she said slightly turning in Cedric's direction.

"I'll have the turkey burger with lettuce, tomato and mayo," he said. "I'll take the potato salad and some water."

"You got it," she said and left their table quickly.

"The service here is pretty fast," he mentioned. "So tell me what you've been up to these last few years," he said trying to break the ice since she was rather quiet.

"I moved around a bit," she said purposely sounding vague. "Now I'm back and just trying to survive," she said. "It's funny seeing you without your glasses. You used to wink at me a lot."

"Actually and honestly, I really wasn't winking on purpose," he confessed. "My glasses were not correct. My mom took me to the clinic to get this huge discount," he recalled. "Well when the glasses were ready, I tried them on and the right eye was perfect, but the left eye was never right. I just kept them, because I didn't want my mom to take off work to start the process over. It caused a little damage for me to wear the glasses for two years, but I survived. I just had to wink to adjust my vision. It was more like a tick," he said.

"I see," she said. She was a little embarrassed to hear the truth.

"How's your brother doing?" Cedric asked to change the subject.

"He's OK, I guess. You know Buster became a firefighter, right?"

"I think I heard Charlie mention that once," he said. "That's great! You must be proud of him."

"I guess it's a good thing to save lives," she said sounding somber. "But everybody's got to die sometime."

"What do you mean?" Cedric asked.

"Well, no one could save my mom, or others who died tragically," she said.

The conversation was starting to sound depressing, so Cedric thought he would turn it around.

"What makes you happy, Melissa?" he asked in a very sincere tone.

"I'll have to think about that," she said. "It's been a long time since I could say I was happy. But once when Buster was visiting, he really made me feel special," she interjected. "He traveled to six states and bought me six different souvenirs. He said it was a big world and he was going to help me to see it one day."

Cedric smiled at the enthusiasm Melissa had when talking about her brother.

THE WAITRESS APPEARED with their food. "Enjoy," she said as she lifted it from the tray and set it before them both.

Cedric bowed his head to say grace quietly. Melissa stared at him and waited for him to finish.

"So are you religious now?" she asked as she took a bite of her burger.

"Some call it religious," he said. "But right now, I'm just thankful."

"Well at least you have something to be thankful for," she said. "Most of the time, life sucks," she continued.

"What?" he said, sounding surprised. "You're a beautiful young woman with a great future ahead," Cedric said.

"What makes you think so?" Melissa asked.

"I just know," he said smiling. "I'm a pretty good judge of character," he continued.

Melissa didn't say much the rest of the meal. She tried to size up Cedric. She wondered if he was as nice as he seemed. She wondered if he could really tell if her future was exciting. She wondered if he really thought she was attractive.

Cedric thanked the waitress and left a nice tip at the end of their lunch. He assisted Melissa into the car and asked her where she would like to be taken.

"Cedric, can you keep a secret?" Melissa asked sincerely. "I've been carrying this secret around for a long time."

"You can trust me," he said looking directly into her face. Then he turned the ignition in the car.

She had a very serious look on her face. Cedric pulled out of his parking space and stopped at the traffic light.

"I think I'm a drug addict," Melissa said.

Chapter Six

CHARLIE HALTED THE MEN in his troop from going in farther. He looked up at the mountains near the Turkey border. He figured this was the best place to rest during the night. It was a small cavern area that would be a great shield against the seasonal rain that had threatened their progress each day.

"Bluford! Ewing!" Charlie called out with natural authority.

"Yes, sir!" both replied simultaneously as they ran to where he was at the front of the cave.

"Go in and check it out!" he said. "Use extreme caution!"

"Yes, sir," Bluford cried out. Ewing nodded and said, "Got it, sir." Ewing pulled out his regulation night vision goggles and put them on. Bluford followed suit and both took the safety off their M24 sniper rifles. The small cave appeared untouched by the undisturbed spider's web at the entrance. The men went in on full alert because in Iraq nothing could be taken for granted.

They were back in three minutes reporting a safe haven. Charlie selected choice men to stand guard in each direction of the cave. The others were to rest and regroup until further orders were given.

Every day he wondered how he ended up as the leader of the platoon. Who could have predicted that the captain of their platoon would get suddenly ill and have to be transported back to the nearest base hospital? That of course left Charlie in charge. He was told it would be a short mission, so he agreed to continue leading the Battalion to the place where the Arabs had a stronghold preventing the U.S. Troops from setting up a much needed command center.

CHARLIE WAS GRATEFUL that it was December. He had heard tales of 125 degree temperatures during the summer months in Iraq.

He pulled out his map and circled their location. At the pace they were going, his company of men would arrive at or near the destination on tomorrow. Until then, they had to be diligent in their watchfulness. The hostile Arabs in this region were not eager to withdraw from the region without a fight.

Charlie ordered the communications soldier to secure a frequency line and report their whereabouts.

"Thanks, Hutson," Charlie said after the young soldier had completed the assignment.

"Can I ask you a question?" Hutson asked in a sound just above a whisper.

"Sure," Charlie answered.

"You gave us soldiers a very convincing talk about this mission," he said almost in a nervous voice. "It's funny that at the time you didn't know you would be leading us. But you said something that really stuck to me. You said you believed the mission was God ordained and sanctioned," he said.

"That's right, Hutson," Charlie interjected. "I can't put my finger on it or explain it very well, but I think we are all in the right place at the right time to do the right thing."

"I just want you to know that I respect your leadership," Hutson continued. "I just wanted, just wanted you to know that no matter what happens," he said.

"Hutson, are you nervous?" Charlie interrupted. "Did something happen that I should know about?

"It turns out we've got something very much in common. See I was talking to Chaplain Bartley," he began, "and he---"

LIEUTENANT HUTSON WAS JUST BEGINNING to open up when he and Charlie both were stunned by the sound of gunfire that seemed to be in their very near vicinity.

Charlie grabbed his weapon and cautiously moved toward the cave opening. He was met by two of the soldiers who were on lookout.

"What is it, soldier?" he asked looking around the perimeters.

"Snipers in the mountains, sir," one of the soldiers reported quickly. "Missed me by a few inches. Must be high-powered equipment at this distance," he continued.

Charlie knew they were close to Mosul but currently pinned down by whoever was taking pot shots from the mountain.

"Attention!" Charlie shouted. "Assume positions," he said.

Each of the soldiers, with weapon in hand, carefully exited the cave and waited for further orders. A shiny reflection that appeared to be a mirror was being flickered back and forth in the mountainous region.

"Either they're trying to blind us or they have other soldiers somewhere in this vicinity," Charlie said to Hutson.

"We may need a scout to see what's directly behind our cave," Charlie said. "Any volunteers?"

The men were vigilant but quiet. Charlie waited another two minutes as the word was repeated around the cave to all the soldiers.

"Hutson," Charlie said strongly. "Get the base on the frequency and let them know we could be surrounded."

Hutson went inside the cave and sent several messages by voice on a secure frequency and by Morse code. Nothing was answered. If they heard the message, they may have thought it too dangerous to respond, or they may not have gotten the message. The various weather changes along with the mountainous terrain could interfere or delay the transmission.

Hutson returned to Charlie's location with a look of gloom.

"Message sent with no response, sir!" Hutson advised. "Shall I repeat the order, sir?" he asked.

"No time," Charlie stated. "I need to find out what's behind this cave. Hutson, keep the men on guard, cautious and observant. My backpack contains the original orders, extra ammo and other important papers. Guard it with your life."

"But, sir," Hutson tried to explain, "I've never…"

38

"That's an order, Hutson."

The attempt to deflect and bow out by Hutson was not to be taken. Charlie went into his backpack and took out several weapons. He also took out a dark powder that he spread on his face. Lieutenant Hutson watched him roll up his sleeves to put more powder on himself. The right shoulder revealed a tattoo with a cupid's arrow through a heart. The camouflage powder was necessary since it was still daylight. He put two grenades in reachable areas and left word to be passed that Hutson would give commands in his absence.

The soldiers covered him as he went behind the cave. They were at the place where the desert ended, and the marshy terrain was only about 100 yards away from their location.

Charlie stayed low and scouted about until he saw where the signal from the glass was actually going. Not more than 50 yards away from a grassy area was a message being sent by the same type of shiny glass.

He crawled closer to the edge and saw that there was a drop off in the land below. Inching closer, he couldn't believe his eyes. There were at least twenty Arabs in enemy uniforms huddled in a section of the land eating. Only one of them was communicating with the enemies in the mountain as far as he could tell. The other shocking sight was the size of the artillery that they had just to the left of where they were.

Charlie stopped to catch his breath and think. He needed to take out both, but they were yards apart.

"The Lord is my shepherd, I shall not want," he mumbled. His head was starting to spin and his thoughts were scattered and not connecting.

"He prepares a table before me in the presence of my enemies." His face fell into his right hand. Could I be sweating in this temperature? he thought to himself.

"Surely, goodness and mercy shall follow me all the days of my life," he concluded.

He reached into the lower leg pocket of his fatigue and grabbed a grenade. He looked for a place to stand where he would not be spotted. Five feet to the west of him was muddy but hidden ground where he could get a good throw. He remembered his soft ball days in junior high.

"Sometimes you only get one chance to throw the winning ball to strike out the opponent," his coach had said to him. "Throw it like your life depends on it," he said.

Charlie was shocked that he could remember this now. He crawled to the spot using his elbows. The grenade was in his right hand.

"I will dwell in the house of the Lord forever," he said as he stood, took aim, pulled the pin and released the grenade.

BAM! THE EXPLOSION WAS STARTLING AND SUCCESSFUL. Now he eyed the artillery. He needed to get closer. He was sure he could do it. He grabbed the grenade and started toward the artillery. The muddy marsh was ankle deep but walkable. Just a few more feet and he'd be there. But he didn't see the shrapnel from the explosion. He removed the pin and attempted to throw the grenade but tripped. His feet got tangled in the remains of the tent material. He thought he felt something on his shoulder and heard a voice but then everything went dark.

It was almost as if the attacks were pre-planned. While the grenade was going off in the marshy, grassy area behind the caverns, helicopters converged in the area. At least two dropped grenades and initiated fire power from the sky. That took care of the hidden snipers in the mountains.

The choppers landed and took aboard each of the troopers. Hutson tried to convince the pilots of the choppers to take a party on a search mission for Charlie. The deliberation was intense but not effective. They had direct orders to land, pick up the men and get out of the area. Intelligence said a wave of enemy Arabs were headed for that location. They would have to try something else to recover Charlie. The choppers did circle the area quickly, hoping to find him, but there was no sign of him and they headed back to the base.

Chapter Seven

CEDRIC TOOK MELISSA HOME. She lived in a small apartment in the not-so-nice part of the city. She refused to tell him anything further. She did give him her phone number and promised to take his call later that evening. She apologized for the sudden outburst, but she told him she could no longer hold it in.

Cedric was like a shell-shocked soldier the rest of the afternoon. His concentration was crucial to his business, but he kept hearing her words in his mind. Who does that? he thought to himself. Who drops a bomb and gives no explanation? He tried to find peace in his mind but could not.

He would apologize later, but after work he went directly to her home. Cedric started to ring the rusty doorbell, but he could see that it didn't work because a piece of heavy duty tape that once covered it was dangling from the bottom.

He tried the outside door and discovered that it was not locked. Once inside, he read the mailboxes.

Atkins, Beeks, Green, Manning, Miller. She was in 204. He cautiously walked up the steps. He had no idea what he would say. He balled his fist to knock and the door opened before his hand hit the wood.

"I've been expecting you," Melissa said. "I happened to be looking out the window and saw you park the car. Why didn't you call me first?" she asked.

"I would have, but I, well I... Melissa, I've been in shock all afternoon. You've got to tell me more. Please tell me what happened."

"Have a seat," Melissa said pointing to her flowered couch. It looked lumpy, but Cedric sat down and waited for her story.

"My life has been one big disappointment," she began. "Nothing has gone right since Mom died," she said. "I'm not the best judge of character, but for some reason, I feel like I can talk to you. Remember that I told you that I lived with my aunt after Mom died? Well that didn't go so well. Her husband was a drunk and was in and out of the home. He and Buster didn't get along very well. So when Buster was old enough, he left. He wanted to take me, but legally he couldn't.

I ran away a few times, but the courts threatened to put me in some juvenile facility because I was a heartache to my aunt. She did the best she could, but she just couldn't control her drunken husband. Anyway," she said, "I got out of there as soon as I turned 18. My uncle died about a year and a half after I left, but I still didn't want to go back."

"Where'd you go?" Cedric asked.

"I had a boyfriend," she said casually. "He turned out to be abusive, so I split." I waited tables for a while, then I got a job as a lunchroom monitor at St. Elizabeth's School," she said. "I was so confused, I even considered joining the convent where the school nuns served," she said laughing. "I just wanted my life to count for something. You know what I mean?" she asked in a despairing way.

"What else happened?" he questioned, trying to keep her on track.

"You'll think I'm horrible, but once I was so depressed that I, I ..."

"Tried to take your own life?" Cedric said, filling in the story.

"Well, yes," she said slowly. "How did you know that?"

"It's not important how I know," he said. "I just do. Go on."

"I had nightmares a lot as a kid," Melissa began. I was always in a building that was on fire or being robbed or drowning or something traumatic. It continued for years. Then one day, after Mom got sick, I watched her take pills to feel better. One day, I went into the medicine cabinet and stole one of her pain pills. It kind of made me sick, but I remember sleeping better. It was like I was in a happy place. I would take several pills at a time and hide them. Mom was too sick to know they were missing, but it set me on a path to an addiction. I didn't know what it was called, but I knew I had to have strong medicine. It continued at my aunt's home. But she didn't have anything that strong. I sometimes had babysitting jobs where I would take from their medicine cabinets. I've tried to quit, but it's so hard. I told myself that I was better than street drug addicts. All my drug use comes from prescription drugs. But I know better. The addiction is just as hard to shake. You know what I mean?" she asked.

Cedric nodded that he understood. "How are you feeding your habit now, Melissa?"

"I was forced to see a doctor a few years ago. When I explained that I couldn't sleep, he ordered a prescription for me and I've never stopped taking it. I know it was supposed to be temporary, but I couldn't make it without this drug," she confessed. "I see normal girls my age enjoying life. Sometimes it makes me feel like I don't have anything to live for at all," she said sobbing into her hands.

Cedric got up and let her cry on his shoulder. "I'll help you, Lissa," he said while she sobbed. "You don't have to face this alone," he continued. "We'll get some help and take care of this whole situation," he said confidently.

"I don't know why I'm opening up to you. Why do you want to help me anyway?" she said wiping her eyes. He handed her a handkerchief and looked directly into her face. "You have value, Melissa. In spite of all the bad things that have happened in your life, you are still greatly loved and valued by God."

"God?" she said as she backed away. "Why did you bring God into this? He doesn't care about me," she said with an attitude.

Cedric smiled gently as if she hadn't said anything. She waited for his response. She was sure he would argue with her the way her aunt did when she was angry with her.

"Well!" she said.

"Is that a statement or a question?" he asked jokingly.

"Aren't you going to tell me that he died on the cross and I should be grateful?" she snapped. "Aren't you going to tell me that there's a heaven and hell and I need to choose. Aren't--"

Cedric cut her off before she could go any further. "I could tell you all of those things," he said. "But it sounds like you already know them. What I will say is this. I don't believe in coincidences. I believe God allowed our paths to cross again for a reason. I'm going to help you, Melissa, but not because I want to save your soul. I can't do that. But like it or not, I care about what happens to my friends. Besides, if I don't help you and my mother finds out, she'll kill me."

Chapter Eight

"TOP OF THE MORNING TO YOU, FOLKS. I'm Captain Reynolds. We're about 10 miles away from Charlotte. Some of you will be departing us at the time of landing and others will be continuing to New York for your final destination. If you're continuing, we're gonna ask you to debark for about 60 minutes while we refuel and restock. Keep your boarding pass handy, and don't go too far from the concourse when we land. So whether you're departing or continuing, the crew and I wish you a safe and happy holiday season."

The flight attendant began to make a final sweep down their aisle to pick up trash and collect pillows no longer needed.

"Sir," she said to Mark, "please put your seat in the upright position."

"What?" Mark said waking up into confusion. "Are we landing?"

"In just a few moments we will be," she said continuing down the aisle.

"New York City here I come," he said peering past Grace and out her window.

"Not quite," Grace said correcting him. "We have to deal with Charlotte first."

"Charlotte who?" he said still rubbing his head.

"North Carolina," Grace said realizing he was in a hangover fog.

"Oh, oh," he said finally understanding the situation.

"I need to call Brian," he said. "I had a bad dream."

Grace resisted the urge to pry. She just smiled and stared out the window. She could see the skyline of the city, thanks to the darkness. A few of the skyscrapers gave a memorable picturesque opportunity for anyone interested in creating a beautiful postcard with their camera.

Mark looked sleepily at Grace. He wondered how much information he had revealed in his intoxicated state. He could only remember bits and pieces.

"I hope I didn't talk you to death," he said. "Unfortunately, it's kind of a blur at this point," he admitted.

"Not at all," she said. "We talked a little and had a great discussion. Thanks for the marriage proposal," she said nonchalantly, "but I'm already taken."

"I proposed?" he said looking confused.

"Got ya!" she said laughing.

MARK CHUCKLED AND LOOKED BACK at his sleepy-eyed friends who seemed to be trying to wake up for the landing.

The flight attendant gave departing instructions and repeated the captain's information about the one hour layover for those continuing to New York.

The debarking passengers entered the Charlotte Douglas International Airport in search of coffee shops.

Grace thought the entire ordeal was interesting. She pondered the significance of knowing someone's personal business when they were a complete stranger. However, she couldn't quite shake the fact that she felt his hurts and pain and rejection. She decided that she would continue to pray for him even though she would never see him again.

THE SMELL OF THE ROASTING COFFEE BEANS led her to the closest cafe. It was still very early in the morning, but she needed a little caffeine. Christmas was still weeks away, but the decorations in the cafe and throughout the concourse were in full swing. Charlotte appears to be expecting Santa Claus, she thought.

Adjacent to the cafe was a bookstore. She saw Santa hats and lots of red scarfs. There were Christmas dolls and trains and even jewelry. Grace's mind immediately began to reminisce about her childhood.

Christmas always looked better in the books than it did in her home. Her parents did the best they could. Her maternal grandparents were immigrants from Cuba and arrived five years before the Cuban Missile Crisis. Her grandmother met and married her grandfather in Little Havana. They thought they would have a better opportunity in New York, so they left Florida shortly afterward.

Her grandfather found a job as a mechanic and her grandmother was a waitress. Life was even harder after their three children were born. Grace's mother was given every opportunity to exceed the education of her parents. She became a nurse's assistant. Due to her contracting arthritis at an early age, she never was able to become a licensed nurse. That's where Grace was favored. From a young child, her mother bought her books about nursing and played games with her about patient care. Then one day, Grace came home from school and told her mother that she wanted to be a nurse.

It was helpful that Spanish was spoken in the house. Graciela was able to get jobs while in school to help translate for her teachers. Many of the classes had children of Hispanic descent.

LOOKING IN THE SHOP at one of the dolls dressed as a nurse prompted many feelings and memories. She remembered the doll that she asked her mother to buy for her. She would have received it for Christmas, but her mother's arthritis took a turn for the worse right after the Thanksgiving holiday. It took all of the money her parents had to get much needed medication. Grace had to rely on the church charity to provide gifts for herself and her little brother.

She removed her eyes away from the toys and focused again on getting some coffee before returning to the airplane. She decided it was best to make a restroom stop before getting the coffee and started scouring out signs for the nearest one. That's when she noticed all of Mark's friends gathered around him. Somehow they all seemed to have sobered up. There was something very somber about their dispositions. There was no laughter or even smiles.

Grace tried not to stare and hurried off to the bathroom. She was pleased that the lines were short. It was probably because it was still early in the morning when few flights are returning or departing. When she returned to the coffee shop, she made a few purchases of sweets that she could eat later, if she became hungry.

She sat in the waiting area and watched the passengers gather. It appeared that the flight would be nearly full for the last part of her journey. Some of the people coming to the waiting area had on winter hats that were now wet. The weather in Charlotte had suddenly changed as it does in winter along the Mid-Atlantic Coast.

"Flight 675 will begin boarding in 15 minutes for New York City," the counter attendant said. A group of nearly 20 Asians stood up and observed the flight number. Their attention went back and forth between their tickets and the flight number posted on the electronic billboard overhead. Grace watched as the man who appeared to be the leader quickly walked to the counter and found out what he had suspected. The attendant pointed down the con-course and gestured to go right. The man, who appeared to be speaking Chinese, bowed his head in either gratitude or to indicate that he understood several times. He motioned for the entire party with him to follow.

Grace hoped in her heart that they didn't miss their flight. She imagined that would be horrible when you are in a foreign place. The attendant asked for parents with young children and any physically challenged passengers to board first. People began hurrying to the area with coffee and food in hand.

GRACE DECIDED that her earlier observation was wrong; the flight was not as full as she thought. It will be good to get home, she thought to herself. She and Buster had planned to spend the holiday together, if it was at all possible. Grace looked forward to this time. She believed this would finally be the Christmas of her dreams.

The passengers appeared scattered throughout the plane. Grace found her window seat and exhaled. She imagined that she was only hours away from relaxing in her comfortable bed. It appeared that all the passengers were aboard. Then there was noise suddenly in the front section of the plane.

"Oh, leave him alone," a man said rather loudly. "He needs time to himself!" he snapped.

Grace looked up and saw Mark's friends boarding loudly. This time they weren't intoxicated. They appeared upset and disgusted.

"I'm gonna ask you to take your seats as quickly as possible," the flight attendant instructed as they passed her coming down the aisle. They didn't respond and continued to talk amongst themselves.

"Biggest waste of time," one of the louder ones said to no one in particular. They seemed to again be assigned or have preferred the back of the plane. Grace closed her eyes and figured perhaps this time she could sleep. In two minutes' time, someone disturbed her and she had to open her tired eyes.

"Is this seat taken?" the passenger asked.

Reluctantly, Grace opened her eyes to find that it was Mark. He didn't appear jovial, but it was clear that he liked something about her. There were clearly other empty seats unclaimed throughout the plane.

"Long time no see," she said teasing.

Chapter Nine

MAJOR BUTLER WEPT QUIETLY with her face buried in her hands. The MIA list was posted, and she read with disbelief that everyone in Charlie's squadron had returned except him.

That made two months in a row that soldiers had gone out on these missions and not everyone had returned. Major Butler didn't know the first soldier that was listed as missing, but this last news seemed to stab her in the heart. She needed to be alone. She headed back to her room. She felt that it always hurt more when you knew the person in peril.

It was her day off work, but it didn't feel that way. She felt lost and confused and desperately needed someone to talk to about her feelings. She turned the corner and headed to her small one room quarters.

"Major Butler!" an unfamiliar voice called out.

She turned and saw a soldier running toward her. He came within two feet and stopped abruptly.

"Hello, ma'am," he said after saluting her. "I have something for you. I'm Lieutenant Hutson. I was with Captain Charlie Grimes the last day he was seen by our squadron. He actually left me in charge," Hutson admitted.

"I've turned everything over to our commander, regarding his weapons and orders," he said. "That is, everything except this," he said, handing her an envelope. "It was inside his backpack," he said softly. He then saluted, turned and left.

For a moment, Major Butler just stood there in shock. She held in her hands an envelope that read 'Bonnie Butler' on the front. Her heart was racing, and she stood there until she could compose herself. She remembered that she was a soldier and held everything inside.

She then found her key and walked a few feet to her front door. She looked around just to be sure that she wasn't being watched and went inside.

She removed the robe from her chair and put it on her bed. Then she sat down and gently opened the envelope.

> *Dear BB,*
>
> *I feel I must write this letter. From the first time I saw you, I knew there was something special about you. I'm not just referring to your beauty, that's obvious to anyone who can see. I love your spirit and your laughter and your personality.*
>
> *I know we have known each other for less than six months, but I feel like I've known you all my life. You are so easy to talk to and to spend time with. There's just one thing that truly bothers me. I want you to get to know my God. I'm a long way from perfect, but I know that our relationship can never really take off the way I would like it to if you don't know Jesus.*
>
> *My ultimate desire is for us to have a marriage relationship and bring great honor to our God and our country.*
>
> *I'm on a very dangerous mission, but I wanted to help to introduce you to my God. A long time ago, a man gave me a ticket to heaven. I know it sounds crazy, but he did. It was just minutes before he actually left to go to heaven. I want to pass my ticket to you. Because once you receive Jesus, you no longer need the ticket.*
>
> *I don't know if we shall see each other again. If you receive this letter, obviously something has happened to me. I wanted to say these things face to face. However, the most important thing is for you to get this ticket. I love you and want you to find me again, even if it is in heaven.*
> *Love Charlie.*

Tears rolled down her face as she completed the letter. She then looked inside the envelope and found a rectangular pamphlet shaped like a ticket that was starting to yellow. It had a permanent crease in the fold. She could tell that it was old and had been preserved through special care.

She read the ticket. Somehow the whole experience seemed surreal. Could this be Charlie's last act of unselfishness? Was he thinking of her while on a dangerous mission? It was too much to take in. She fell to her knees sobbing.

"Oh Charlie, Charlie, Charlie," she said. "Dear God," she said. "Please send him back to me," she sobbed. "I promise that I really do believe in you. You are the true God," she said between sobs. "Just help me, help me, help me."

Chapter Ten

CEDRIC LET THE PHONE RING at least six times, but there was no answer. He hung up and tried again. Melissa picked up on the second ring, sounding out of breath.

"Hey Lissa, are you ok?" he asked.

"Sure, why are you asking?" she questioned.

"You just sound out of breath," he said.

"I was in the shower when I heard the phone ringing," she answered. "You really don't have to worry about me every hour of the day," she snapped. "I'm a big girl."

Cedric remained silent on the phone.

"I'm sorry Cedric," she said apologizing. "I'm a little touchy whenever I try to wean myself from the pills."

"I've got some good news for you, Lissa," he said. "I've been in touch with a non-profit group that specializes in helping those who are involved in substance abuse. Now hear me out before you make any judgment. The group has a proven track record for helping those who take advantage of their program. They just need you to give them 21 days. Now, Lissa, that might seem like a long time, but your body is like a computer system that needs to be worked on and then rebooted."

Melissa stood and held the phone. She wanted to do it, but she was scared. She didn't like isolation or being controlled by others. She wanted to be free of the huge, silent monster that followed her everywhere she went. How many times had she tried to do this on her own? How many times did she promise herself that she wouldn't take another pill? How many times did she tell herself that everybody had demons? There were too many times, and too many excuses to count.

She had lost all her friends because they couldn't trust her. She was miserable and wished on a number of occasions that she could just go to sleep and never wake up again. The only thing that really bothered her was her brother. She loved Buster and he loved her. She didn't want to break Buster's heart. He was her real family.

Then Melissa dared to hope. She tried to remember what it felt like to really be free. She could barely remember. So she stood there and imagined herself having a normal conversation with normal people. She would not have to excuse herself when she started shaking. She wouldn't get the urge to ramble through the medicine cabinet of strangers or friends. She might even someday become an asset to society instead of a nuisance. Boy did being free sound like a million dollars.

"OK, I'll do it," Melissa said. The words sounded strange coming out of her mouth.

"You will?" Cedric said getting excited. He expected a fight. He thought he was going to have to talk a long time to convince her.

"When do I start?" she said.

Chapter Eleven

"I DON'T MEAN TO BOTHER YOU," Mark said. "But I can't really face my buddies right now," he explained.

"I understand," Grace replied.

"Actually, you don't," Mark continued. "You see, well, Brian just called off the marriage," he admitted while searching her face for a reaction.

Grace used her best poker face. Inside she was glad it was called off; she did, however, feel sorry for Mark. She wasn't sure what to say in reaction to those words. In her heart she asked the Lord to help her. Maybe she could be of comfort to this young man who was clearly confused and hurting.

"Mark," she began, but paused to try to find the right words. "There's a song that I love written by a man named Michael W. Smith. The words seem to speak to my soul," she continued.

"In the song he says, "I'm looking for a reason, roaming through the night to find my place in this world, my place in this world, not a lot to lean on, I need your light to help me find my place in this world, my place in this world."

"So, have you found your place in this world, Grace?" he asked softly, choking back emotion.

"I believe I have," she said. "While none of us really know exactly what the future will bring, I trust in my God who has already measured my future and walked it out. I just have to follow in his footsteps."

"Are you sure you're on the right path?" he said almost sarcastically.

"Oh, I know that my path is correct," she said. "I have a wonderful young man who pursued me until I completely fell in love with him. I never knew anybody so kind could love me unconditionally.

But then I understood more about the kind of love God has for all of us when I accepted the love of Buster," she said smiling.

"I wouldn't know anything about that," Mark lamented. "Someone else came along and Brian just changed his mind."

"Mark, I know I don't know you that well, but I truly believe God has a different plan for your life," she said.

"Well, I wish he'd reveal it," he said. "Not that I really believe in him. Although, I know there's something greater than me out there," he said, looking out the window.

"Perhaps today is the day that he starts to reveal his plan," she said. "Even in situations that we don't understand."

THEY CONTINUED TO TALK during the instructions for safety, and when Grace finished speaking the plane began to take off.

When the flight attendant made her rounds, Grace declined any snacks. She had hoped to sleep on the earlier flight, but that didn't happen. This was her second chance.

"What's it like to really be in love?" Mark asked. "Seems like every time I think I've been accepted for who I am, the rug is pulled from under me. I don't know that I really have a safe place in this world. People are so deceptive. They use you until they use you up. I think I'm gonna order a drink," he said.

"Well to answer your question about love, I can only tell you what I've discovered," Grace said. "This is a fallen world; nothing about it is perfect. You know. But there are glimpses of goodness all around us. I see love in a beautiful flower or a newborn baby. I look out this window and see the beautiful clouds floating by. I've experienced tragedy in my family, but I know that I can't focus on the tragedy. Somehow I feel that, because I am still here, the hand of God is guiding me to a better place. And since I know that, I have this love for God that I can't quite explain. This love for him is much deeper than my love for Buster."

She went into her purse to pull out her special ticket.

"That's why this ticket means so much to me. Especially this section about acknowledging Jesus. You know, this may sound unbelievable. But the day I was stuck in the elevator, the fire department had another call just 30 seconds earlier. Buster was suiting up for the first call, then the captain decided to take that one and sent Buster to me. I know it had to be the providence of God. This ticket is the answer to emergency …"

MARK SEEMED TO BE hanging on every word. But just as she began to talk to him about the ticket, the plane shook with a jolt that caused the ticket to fly up in the air. They both tried to catch it, but then the captain came on the PA to announce weather disturbances that were causing turbulence. The ticket flew behind them and the fasten seatbelt sign appeared.

Grace and Mark both made sure their seatbelts were secure while looking out the window. The clouds seemed to race by instead of floating and there was more rocky riding. The plane began jerking and a jolt pushed their heads back and seemed to hold them there. Simultaneously, the plane began to climb at what appeared to be a sixty degree angle. A few gasps and curses from passengers were released with the sudden speed and tilt of the plane. Then just as suddenly as it had climbed at the steep level, it reversed and seemed to descend at the same degree angle. In the middle of the confusion and to Mark's surprise, the man behind him stuck his long arm out and handed Mark the ticket.

"You dropped something," he said as he put the ticket over Mark's shoulder and let it fall on his lap. The man whistled a calming tune. Mark opened his closed eyes and saw clearly the words on the ticket. In spite of the descent of the plane, he could clearly read one section of the ticket. He read it silently amidst moans and screams and shock around him. He read it until the plane's lights flickered and finally went into total blackness. He read it and somehow released his fear and believed.

Chapter Twelve

GENERAL GALSTER LEFT THE MESS HALL and headed straight to his officer's meeting. He entered the room in relatively good spirits. He was quite surprised by the sullen looks of the other officers.

"At ease, men," General Galster said after saluting the eighteen officers. He pulled a report from the black military issued briefcase and stood in front of a podium.

"I have here a complete report of the recent reconnaissance mission carried out on 12 December," he said. "Seventy-five percent of the necessary information has been obtained. I can't remember a mission where I was any prouder of the platoon," he said. "All but one of the soldiers is safe and accounted for, and I think that's worth celebrating," he said smiling.

"Excuse me, General," Lieutenant General Lincoln said, interrupting. "We have a soldier that's MIA. Actually two, if you include the mission from September," he said. "I reserve the right to celebrate when their families are able to celebrate."

"I meant no disrespect to the missing soldiers," General Galster said. "I'm just looking at the bigger picture. It's an endless desert out there. We don't know if we shall ever know what has happened to either soldier. In the meantime, I feel it's our duty to congratulate those who were careful and diligent in their mission."

"Just a minute, General," Lieutenant General Lincoln persisted. "I've listened to the verbal preliminary reports of the men, including the soldier left in charge. I would like to submit the name of Captain Charlie Grimes for hero status, pending his return."

"Oh, let's not be premature in our submissions, General," General Galster said. "There's an entire process that must vet his disappearance.

Personally, I find it quite odd that he could not be found considering the open terrain in the immediate vicinity of their holding place of refuge."

"General, are you suggesting that his disappearance was calculated?" Lieutenant General Lincoln questioned.

"Officers, let me be clear. None of us know the whereabouts of our missing Captain. What we do know is that some previous missions indicate some of our men may have been sympathetic to the enemy. Whenever that happens, you never know where a soldier's loyalty lies," he said emphatically.

The officers listened with disbelief. General Galster all but accused Captain Grimes of treason. This particularly bothered Chaplain Bartley. He knew when rumors of this sort escaped, it lessened the chance of soldiers searching wholeheartedly for the MIA.

GENERAL GALSTER DISMISSED THE MEETING. He had accomplished his secret desire to plant some doubt in the minds of those who adored the Captain. Chaplain Bartley left the meeting angry and saddened. He went to his office and grunted a greeting at Major Butler as he passed her desk.

She quickly put away the tissue that she was using to wipe her intermittent tears that seemed to just drop involuntarily at different times of the day. She followed him into his office and stood in front of his desk.

"Chaplain Bartley, I need help," she said softly trying to restrain herself.

"How can I help you?" he said wondering why she seemed despondent.

"I'm not sure you are aware that Captain Grimes and I had been seeing each other," she said as boldly as she could.

"Well, I've seen the way he's looked at you, but I had no idea it was serious. Please, have a seat," he said gesturing toward his visitor's chair. "Let me offer my sincerest wishes that the Captain is found very soon. I'm sure that this ordeal is very difficult for you."

She lowered her head and sighed while sitting in the chair.

"You know, Chaplain Bartley, sometimes it just doesn't work when you play the hard to get game," she said.

"What do you mean?" he said.

"I think I took it for granted that Charlie, excuse me, the Captain would be around to woo me and court me or date me or whatever," she said. "But I just got a wake-up call. Tomorrow is not promised to any of us. I just want the chance to make it right," she said.

"I'll pray that you get that opportunity," he said smiling.

HIS SMILE REMINDED HER OF HER DAD. There were times that only her father seemed to be able to help her. His wisdom seemed enormous when she was young. The Chaplain had so many similar traits except he had one that her father did not pass on. Her father was not big on religion.

"Speaking of prayer, can you help me with one other thing?" she asked. She dropped her head while speaking, looking totally embarrassed. "Can you help me find my way to God?" she asked with her voice quivering to hold back the overwhelming emotion that she had bottled up inside.

"Aren't you already a believer?" he questioned. The entire time she worked in his office, he never questioned her faith. It actually was not his job to do so, and she never appeared to be searching from what he had observed.

"I was a slow bloomer, but I am a believer now," she said as her courage seemed to increase.

"Well, you're almost there," he said smiling. "Anybody who comes to God must first believe that he exists," he said. "If you have faith to believe in the Invisible God, he honors that faith and will begin a relationship with you that he will develop on his terms so that you can grow and get stronger in that faith. I want to read a passage to you," he said pulling his Bible from his desk drawer as he had done so many times before.

"Here it is, Romans the tenth chapter and verses eight through ten.

'But what does it say? The word is near you, in your mouth and in your heart' (that is, the word of faith which we preach): that if you confess with your mouth the Lord Jesus and believe in your heart that God has raised Him from the dead, you will be saved. For with the heart one believes unto righteousness, and with the mouth confession is made unto salvation.'"

Chaplain Bartley read the scripture with renewed confidence. The anger he felt against General Galster seemed to have dissipated from the room. He didn't know if Charlie was dead or alive, but clearly if he was dead, his impact on this one person would follow him into eternity.

"Are you ready to make this confession?" he asked.

"I'm ready to join God's army," she said with a smile.

Chapter Thirteen

THE CUSTOMER SHOOK CEDRIC'S HAND with such enthusiasm. Cedric had solved the mystery of the location of the safety deposit box. The customer had found the key when his wife died and had no clue what the key would unlock. He actually had no clue to what bank the key belonged. Cedric could only confirm certain information by law. However, he could identify the key to their safety deposit boxes because they were unique. After a private system of determining what box it fit, Cedric steered the widower to the right box.

The savings bonds inside were gifts of the parents of the deceased. She had never cashed them in. The gentleman was ecstatic and overwhelmed with gratitude.

Cedric was pleased that he could be helpful to good people. He returned to his desk to complete paperwork. The shadow of an individual caused him to look up to find a well-dressed gentleman in front of his desk.

"May I help you with something?" he asked.

"I'd like to ask you a few questions," the man said as he flipped a badge with his identification showing.

"Sure," Cedric answered.

"I'd like to see the account of Melissa Miller," he said.

"Um, sure detective," Cedric said trying to be discreet. "I just need to see your warrant," he said.

"I don't have it with me, but I can have it in a few hours," the detective said. "Is there any reason for you not to cooperate with me now?" the detective said.

"Three reasons," Cedric answered. "It's against bank policy, it's against state regulation and it's against federal law. But I'm sure you already know that, right?"

"Look, young man, the FBI is involved in this matter, and I'm sure they appreciate your diligence to following rules, but time is of the essence. There's a hot lead that led to this bank, and we intend to get what we're looking for."

"I understand," Cedric said. "Let me make a call to our bank president."

The detective's eyes followed Cedric as he pulled a card from inside his top right drawer that had a number written on a gold foil business card.

"Good afternoon, Mr. Bennington. This is Cedric Grimes at Silver Linings Bank. I have a detective here requesting permission to see a customer's account. Yes. Yes, I did. Yes, he is. I'll do it right away, sir."

The detective smiled as Cedric hung up the phone.

"He told me to let you know you can have my complete cooperation once you produce the warrant."

The detective's eyes seemed fiery as he left in anger, and Cedric knew that would not be the last time he would be approached for the information.

Now Cedric was concerned. Why would a detective want to see Melissa's account? he wondered.

He wasn't allowed to call her. She was in rehab. He would have to wait this one out. In his heart, he prayed that she wasn't in any real trouble. But if she was, he was determined to help her, no matter what.

Chapter Fourteen

THERE WAS A BUZZING SOUND followed by crackling, and then the flickering lights returned. The plane steadied as it abruptly ended its descent to a slow soar and balanced itself in the stratosphere. Mark slowly opened his eyes unsure if he was dead or alive.

"I'm alive. I'm actually alive!" he said with excitement. Mark turned toward Grace, who was wiping the sweat from her brow with the back of her right hand. The entire plane was abuzz with passengers crying to cheering.

"Thank you, Jesus," Grace said looking up. She realized that this was a close call. Her eyes fell on the ticket that Mark held in his hand. He made a move to give it back to her, but her hand grabbed his and prevented him from giving it back.

"The ticket is yours," she said softly. The captain was starting to explain what happened to the plane in the weather turbulence. She chose to ignore his explanation and continue her conversation with Mark. "I've already made my peace with God," she said in a matter of fact manner.

Mark began wondering if reading the ticket had spared his life or if this whole incident was a coincidence.

However, deep in his heart of hearts, he was sure that it was not a coincidence. He had asked God in a non-verbal voice to give him another chance. He wasn't sure he could even call it a prayer because his lips never moved. What seemed like an eternity had only been a few minutes. For a few moments, he felt like God had his undivided attention. Not only that, but he thought during that brief period that he heard God speak to him. He said that if he survived the ordeal, that would be proof enough that God was real. But this was extra special. Was God actually speaking to him directly? Mark looked around for his friends and saw that the flight attendants were checking on them. He could see the face of one of his friends, and he looked as if he had seen a ghost.

"Are you sure you're alright?" he asked Grace. The flight attendant arrived at their row almost immediately after he asked and said the same words.

"I'm a nurse," Grace said responding to the flight attendant. Please let me know if I can help in any way."

"That's good to know," the attendant said. "One of our passengers on Row 31 may have had a seizure according to the passenger next to him," the attendant said. "Of course, he denies it, because you don't remember a seizure," she continued. "If I need you to take his vitals, I'll come back," she said. "Thanks for your willingness to help."

AS THE ATTENDANT CONTINUED moving toward the passengers on the row across from them, Grace did a double look at Mark. She looked directly in his face.

"Mark, are you sure you're ok? Your face has a certain glow," Grace insisted.

Mark took a deep breath. "Something has happened to me, Grace," he said with a sincere tone. "I think God has spoken to me," he said. "I feel a great sense of uh, well, peace."

He then excused himself and went to the rear bathroom.

Grace sat in her seat frozen. She wondered if God was answering the prayer she had prayed just hours ago. She did not expect his answer to her prayer to take place that quickly. She bowed her head in gratitude and whispered a prayer of thanksgiving.

Mark barely made it to the lavatory before he burst into shameless tears. He cried from a deep place within him. It was a place that had been sheltered from any emotions since he was a child. It was a place he had reserved to only reveal to the person who loved him unconditionally. He didn't know it before now, but it was a place that only God could dwell and heal and bring into peace. It was a cry of finally

66

knowing that God truly did exist and knew who he was and still loved him. It was a cry he had wanted to release for most of his life. So there in the lavatory of that airplane, Mark was transparent and vulnerable. He didn't care. Today was the day he began his journey to wholeness.

Chapter Fifteen

MELISSA FELT A PRESENCE IN HER ROOM. She knew who it was. It was dark and she couldn't reach the light switch. Yet she could smell the body odor of her visitor. Why didn't someone help her? Why couldn't they see through his charm? This time she would let out a yell before he got near her. She mustered up the biggest scream she could find. It filled the night air and bounced around the room and through the heating ventilation system.

"Ms. Melissa! Ms. Melissa!" a voice said trying to calm her.

"He's in here again," Melissa cried. "He tried to touch me again," she insisted while holding on to the iron headboard.

"No one is here, Ms. Melissa," the attendant said reassuringly. "It was just another bad dream. No one can hurt you here. You're having withdrawal symptoms. But you will be fine," she said.

"I want my mother," Melissa wept as she hugged the tear-stained pillow as tightly as she could. "Mommy, why did you leave me? I need you to be with me," she sobbed. "I can't stay here without you, Mommy. Oh, Mommy, come back to me," she begged.

"Melissa, Melissa listen to me," the attendant said using a stronger voice to get her attention. "Your mother is deceased. I'm sorry, but she is. You're getting the help that you need to overcome your drug dependency. Soon you will be free and there will be no trace of those demons in your system. In the meantime, I want you to calm down so you can prepare for dinner. A hot meal will help you feel better."

Melissa began shaking uncontrollably. She then looked at the attendant as if she had seen a ghost. She began backing away from her and cowered in a corner. She let out a subdued scream then seemed to fall into a deep sleep.

The attendant shook her head. "Poor thing," she said as she

backed out of the room and locked the door.

She quickly returned to her office to write down her notes.

She found the last page she had written on and included the findings of the day.

DAY THREE–Evidence of molestation and unresolved issues with deceased mother. Hallucinations commonly associated with withdrawals from opioids and unknown illegal stimulants.

Melissa's deep sleep was not a peaceful one. She was again a little girl craving her mother's attention. She did her best to explain to her mother that she didn't like her boyfriend. "But he likes you, Lissa," her mother would say.

"He likes me too much, Mommy!" Melissa would say. Her mother would laugh and say, "That's so sweet! Lissa, you're too cute!"

Melissa was at a loss. She didn't know how to communicate that she was being touched inappropriately. Her mom thought it was entertaining when her boyfriend Marvin tickled her daughter.

Melissa would sometimes scream, and her mother would tell her to stop showing off. Those repeated rebukes caused her to be withdrawn and an introvert. She sometimes only spoke to her imaginary friend Tina. Tina was easy to talk to and told her that she wasn't a bad person.

The telephone rang and interrupted the attendant's paperwork. "Open Door Sanctuary," she answered.

'Hello, my name is Bernard Miller. I'd like to speak to my sister, Melissa Miller."

"Hello, Mr. Miller. This is Ms. Smith. Due to our rules and policies, I need you to verify a few things before I can release any information. Let's see. She chose three questions to identify her if there were any calls," she said, reading from the file she had pulled from the drawer.

"What's the date of birth, her birthmark and her mother's maiden name?" she asked.

"March 15, a strawberry and Singleton," he answered.

"You answered correctly," she said with relief. "I apologize for the delay, but you'd be surprised at the people who want to do harm to our residents during their stay," she said. "I'm the attendant for your sister. She is not quite in a position to take calls at this time. She's in the middle of the crucial window of time that it takes to overcome her addiction."

"Addiction? So this is not a hospital?" he said shocked.

"Sir, I thought you understood. What is it that your sister told you?"

"She left me a voicemail saying she had to go into the hospital for a few days for tests, just in case I couldn't reach her. She left this number for emergency purposes. I had no idea," he said.

"Please don't tell anyone I told you," she said nervously. "I don't want to lose my job. I thought when you answered all the questions you were aware of what was going on."

"What kind of addiction?" he asked.

"I'm afraid I can't answer any more questions," she said nicely. "But your sister is getting the care that she needs."

"I'm in another state," he said. "But I will be there as soon as I can."

Buster hung up the phone and just stared at the ceiling of the firehouse.He would have to work three more days before his normal five days off. He felt shocked in one way, but not in another. He immediately blamed Melissa's boyfriend whom he had never met. She often talked about him and said she would leave him when things went wrong. Buster wanted so badly to have Melissa join him in New York.

She was determined to make it on her own, so he went along with her plans. He now saw that it was a mistake. She was much too young to make crucial decisions like that. He knew she didn't want to stay with their aunt, but he thought her job could both sustain her and keep her out of trouble.

He wasn't sure what to do. He wondered if the addiction was heroin or crack cocaine or something as horrible as meth. He had seen the results of such an addiction too often in his line of work. By the time the fire department was called, a meth lab would often be inflamed. Or he would have to use the jaws of life to rescue some poor kid who overdosed and tried to drive through a brick wall.

He put his hands over his ears as if he could stop the horrible ideas from entering his head. Then he remembered. At his last visit to church, his pastor read a passage about the heart being overwhelmed. Buster had taken some notes, but they were in his apartment. He knew it was in the Psalms. He picked up his cell phone and googled overwhelmed heart. He was immediately taken to Psalm 61:2. He read the verse and decided to read the entire eight verses of that Psalm. Just as he was beginning to calm his nerves from the disturbing news, a blasting alarm sounded that caused him to drop his phone. He picked up the phone and joined his crew in seconds as they donned their rubber boots and fire retarding gear. For the moment, he would put his family crisis on hold and attend to a stranger's call for help.

Chapter Sixteen

CEDRIC HEARD NOTHING BUT SOBBING when he picked up his home phone. He picked it up quickly because the ringing was disturbing the news broadcaster's reveal of the final score for his favorite basketball team. He didn't have time to check the caller id. He had fallen asleep and missed the last 20 minutes of the game. He woke just in time to hear the score. He blamed it on his antihistamine. Nearly every December he seemed to get attacked with a cold.

He muted the sound of the television. Something very serious had happened, but he couldn't determine what it was. "Slow down," he said. "I can't understand what you're saying. Who is this?" he said, standing and searching the ceiling fan for answers.

"It's, it's," was all he heard.

"Mom?" he asked. "What's wrong? Are you alright?"

"They called," she said breaking down again.

"Who called?" Cedric asked.

"The army," she answered, finally able to compose herself. "He's missing," she whispered wiping her tears. "Your brother is missing in action."

Finally the words escaped her lips.

"What can we do, Mom?" Cedric asked finally understanding the barrage of tears.

"The army will be searching daily, but I was told that the land is so vast it's like looking for a needle in a haystack," she said.

CEDRIC SHOOK HIS HEAD IN DISBELIEF. He did not know what to say or think. He knew when his brother joined the military, there was a chance of this or something worse happening.

Cedric sighed and took a deep breath. "I'll be over in a few minutes."

He hung up the phone and sat down on the tall chair pulled against his kitchen counter. He wanted to cry, but the tears would not come. He was very close to his brother. When something was wrong with Charlie, he could always sense it when they were growing up. He found it so strange that he had not sensed anything unusual. Perhaps it was because he had been involved in the problems of Melissa. He was sure that was it.

He looked around the apartment. It was such a great place to live. It's strange that the status of a great place to live and work is not very important when you have a family crisis. Vacation Bible School came to his mind. He and Charlie knew so little about Jesus until they were invited to attend the VBS in their neighborhood.

It was there that they were introduced to Jesus. It was there that they were able to cope with the tragedy they had witnessed at a young age. He wasn't quite sure why they stopped going after three years. As he recalled, the church stopped offering the program. Then his mind went to the summer concert when they were teens. Charlie's friend Alex, a bold Christian leader in high school, invited him to come. Charlie said he would go if his brother could go. Alex's dad picked them up and took them to the outdoor concert. The music was addictive, but the lyrics were powerful.

AT THE END OF THE CONCERT, young people were giving their lives to Jesus and renewing their relationship with him too. That's when Charlie stood to go up and Cedric followed. A tear seemed to fall from Cedric's eye as he remembered that this was the best decision he had ever made. It was then that he appreciated the ticket that he had never parted with. He knew that he had an invitation to heaven that began the day he innocently went to the park with his family.

The telephone rang again and interrupted his memories. This time he looked at the caller ID.

"Hey, Mom," he answered.

"Cedric," Rachel said with a lot less emotion than a few moments earlier. "I forgot to tell you that I was contacted by an old friend. You'll never guess who's trying to reach you."

"I'm sure you're right," he said sounding like he didn't want to play a guessing game.

"I got a call from little Buster, Christina's son. It was so good to hear from him," she said sniffling. He said that Melissa's in some type of rehab. Poor thing. He's coming here to our city to check on her. You know he lives in New York. He said when he last spoke with Melissa, she mentioned you. Is that right? You've seen Lissa?" she asked.

"As a matter of fact, I have," he said. "I'll be over soon to tell you all about it," he said before hanging up. Wow, he thought, my childhood is visiting me in more than one way. His mind was heavily on his brother. He cared about Melissa, but he knew she was in a safe place. He was now concerned with whether his brother was dead or alive, hurt or safe, scared or being brave.

Chapter Seventeen

LIEUTENANT HUTSON HAD ONE HOUR LEFT to patrol through the Kurdish village marketplace. His convoy would meet him at the end of the shift. His assignment was to keep a close watch on the people.

A thousand thoughts filled his mind. He wondered how he ended up on the other side of the world. It's not that the cultures clashed, but they were worlds apart. He walked from table to table in the market. He saw many goats, sheared lamb's wool made into coats, cucumbers and bread from cracked wheat.

He also saw colorful clothing pieces and little trinkets. He noticed a darling little Kurdish girl sitting at one of the tables playing. She held something shiny in her hands that was magnified by the sun. Lieutenant Hutson's curiosity caused him to look closer. He stopped sharply as if he had been wounded by a dagger. The little girl was swinging dog tags back and forth on silver chains.

He nearly grabbed them from her hand but was hesitant because of the watchful eye of her father. He pointed to the tags and tried to get the father to understand his interest. Then he pulled his own from beneath his clothing so he could see that it was American property.

The language barrier made it difficult to find out where they got them from. The father finally allowed Lieutenant Hutson to inspect the dog tags. He read them both and asked if anyone spoke English. When no one responded to his language, he resorted to the few simple words the troopers had been taught when deployed to that country. "Saa' adinii! Saa' adinii!" he repeated. He figured if they didn't understand the word 'help,' they wouldn't understand anything. He said it louder while looking around, until one of the other men from three booths away came down to offer assistance.

"Soldier need help?" he said in broken English.

Lieutenant Hutson was so relieved he could have hugged the man. "Yes," Lieutenant Hutson said excitedly. "Please ask the little girl's father where she got these," he said holding the dog tags in the air.

He witnessed the man engaging the child's father in either Arabic or the Kurdish language. They seemed to go back and forth for a long time in Lieutenant Hutson's mind. He was anxious to get to the bottom of the situation. The man finally turned to the trooper with an explanation.

"His daughter got from boy at village two day ago," he said holding up two fingers.

"This village?" the trooper asked.

"No, village in mountain," he said. He then turned to point to the mountains behind them.

REMEMBERING THE DIPLOMACY RULES, he asked the man to find out two things: What will he take in exchange for the items and would they take him to their village.

The exchange did not seem to go well. The father seemed to look at the soldier as if he were now the enemy. Lieutenant Hutson thought he should intervene. One thing the Kurdish people valued was animals.

"Tell him he's not in any trouble. I will buy him a lamb for the dog tags," he said. "If he takes us to his village and helps find the soldier who wore these tags, I will also give him a cow," he promised.

That began another extensive conversation. The father appeared, from Lieutenant Hutson's point of view, to again become friendly.

"Soldiers not always truthful," the man said in broken English. "What have you now for trade?"

Lieutenant Hutson was not sure what to do. As he deliberated, he noticed his fellow soldiers in a jeep headed toward him down the narrow market street as goats scurried off and chickens ran away.

"Wait here," he said to the father and interpreter. He proceeded to discuss his findings with the men. One jumped out of the jeep ready to engage in what could have been a confrontation. Lieutenant Hutson convinced them that taking the dog tags forcibly was not good for army-civilian relations. Instead, they each contributed several American dollars. Villagers knew where to exchange the funds for their own currency. It usually was a great sign of faith to give them money because they really were dirt poor.

One of the soldiers called the command post and told them of Lieutenant Hutson's discovery. The commanding officer insisted they wait till the next morning to invade the mountains for safety purposes. He said he would get a squadron ready at 0600 hours and to reconnect with the villager at that time. The excitement of the money caused the villager to commit to being there at first light and to promise to take them to the mountain village.

Chapter Eighteen

THE MESS HALL WAS NOTICEABLY EMPTY of ranking officers. This was quite unusual for a day that they were not on high alert. Something was up. Major Butler knew it and made a remark to one of the other servicemen.

"Where is everybody?" she said casually as she sat down at the officers table.

"I heard a couple of dog tags were found in the marketplace today," a fellow soldier whispered as a response. "But you didn't hear that from me," he said looking around.

Major Butler was afraid to ask more questions. It was not a good sign when a dog tag was found. Grenades were leading causes of dog tags showing up in strange places. If a soldier's boot was lost, stolen or blown off, his secondary dog tag was often found.

She knew whatever was going on would be considered classified information. Yet her years in the army had taught her that nothing had remained top secret very long since the Cold War. There were too many disloyal participants who didn't understand the meaning of the words top secret.

Hearing the news of the found dog tags took the appetite away from her immediately. She simply said, "Excuse me," to the three people sitting at her table, took her tray and left it on the conveyor belt.

She went back to her quarters and paced the floor. What if they've found Charlie's dog tags? she thought. She dismissed the idea. She didn't want them to find his dog tags. She wanted them to find him. But don't let them just find him, she prayed internally. Let him be alive.

She turned to get her bedclothes for the evening. But there was a flash of light that passed her window. She attempted to walk toward the window when a siren was released. It was an emergency siren. It had only happened once since she was deployed to this site. She spontaneously dropped to the floor and remembered that she was not in America. She was at war in a foreign country. She stayed on the floor to listen for another siren. The one they used to get the soldiers underground. The siren never happened. Instead there was an all-clear alarm that sounded.

She got up and went to get a towel. Her nerves were on edge. For the first time in a long time, she felt scared and uncertain. She wanted to call her family, her friends and the Chaplain. But of course he would be busy with orders.

SHE LOOKED AGAIN OUT THE WINDOW into the mountains. A few glaring lights were visible. She did not confuse them with lightning. She prayed and backed away from her window. The American allies, she recalled, would sometimes send flares at night when they discovered enemy strongholds in the mountains.

She felt nervous and fearful. The uncertainty of everything she faced was too much. For some reason, Major Butler believed that if she read the Bible, she would feel better. The tiny library on her base was not open at this time. Then she remembered. The Gideon's had mailed Bibles to her base many months earlier. When they were distributed, she had no intention of reading it. Now she wanted to read it more than anything.

She thought hard and finally smiled as if a light had gone on in her head. She went to her closet and pulled out a box. It was taped up and marked to be shipped. The Major systematically removed the tape without ripping the box. She removed a few souvenirs that she had purchased from the village. There beneath the souvenirs was a special edition of the Holy Bible. Due to her lack of a Christian up-bringing, she had never felt the need to use the Bible daily. Yet she had felt strange about discarding it. When she had considered it, her conscious wouldn't allow it. She believed that someone would know and consider her a heathen.

She didn't know where to start. "Lord, help me!" she spoke aloud. She wished she had the knowledge of the Chaplain. Then she looked at the table of contents and saw all the books. She was considering picking one by using her age. She could pick book 26. That would be Ezekiel. His name put her in remembrance of the song she learned as a child. Ezekiel saw a wheel way up in the middle of the air. That caused a smirk on her face. I never understood that song, she thought to herself. She continued to consider different numbers like her birth month or the day of the month she was born. She wondered if she should add them together.

She nearly scrapped the entire ordeal when another sound from far in the distance broke the silence. It startled her, and she dropped the Bible. When she reached to retrieve it, there was a purple bookmark protruding from the center of the book. The heading read: Where to Find Help when Facing Life's Issues. She let her finger follow the categories and her finger rested on 'When Feeling Afraid– Psalm 121.'

Major Butler looked again in the index to find Psalm. When she had located Psalm 121, she read the entire chapter.

1 *I will lift up mine eyes unto the hills, from whence cometh my help.*
2 *My help cometh from the Lord, which made heaven and earth.*
3 *He will not suffer thy foot to be moved: he that keepeth thee will not slumber.*
4 *Behold, he that keepeth Israel shall neither slumber nor sleep.*
5 *The Lord is thy keeper: the Lord is thy shade upon thy right hand.*
6 *The sun shall not smite thee by day, nor the moon by night.*
7 *The Lord shall preserve thee from all evil: he shall preserve thy soul.*
8 *The Lord shall preserve thy going out and thy coming in from this time forth, and even for evermore.*

An indescribable calm came over Major Butler. She smiled and looked toward the window where the majestic mountains had caused her such tension. She felt now like the very God of the mountains had brought peace to her. She dropped her head and did something she had never done before. She prayed to God for a miracle and made a special vow.

Chapter Nineteen

MELISSA SAT AT THE DINNER TABLE and shared a laugh with the other three women. They all battled some form of addiction. Perhaps that's why she felt at ease. She was in the company of those who understood what it felt like to be a prisoner in your own body. On the outside it looked like you had self-control. Melissa had mastered the game of pretense. She appeared to be a person in control of her body. She certainly believed she was at times. Deep down, she was convinced that she controlled everything except her will.

Two days earlier, she thought she was losing her mind. There was one black dot on her floor that kept moving. Melissa had compared notes with some of the other girls. They concluded that hallucinations were worse than anything. For instance, the black dot kept getting closer and closer to her. Even in her messed up condition, she tried to will her mind to see correctly.

She was, of course, shocked when Ms. Smith came in her room and killed the moving dot. It was a real spider after all. That's when she knew her sanity was returning.

It wasn't until after the laughter had escaped her that she paused to realize that she felt whole again. It had been a long time coming. She wasn't sure how she had continued to go day after day living in an invisible prison. She had only been able to go as far as her addiction allowed her to go. She was the puppet on the end of her addiction's string.

Many days she had to convince herself that her life would get better. Her addiction would behave for a number of days and then take a nosedive. She fooled herself many times. If she went three days without her pills, she told herself she would never touch them again.

It was a miserable roller coaster ride. She would go to work and put on a facade. She left work early on many days unable to cope. She tried to use mind control over her condition. That didn't work. She was told at clinics that she had a disease. She never agreed with that. How could she have a disease that she had brought upon herself? What she actually had was an addiction, and she wanted to finally be honest with herself. No more games. She wanted to go forward in her life. So far it had been pretty miserable.

She smiled and decided that she would join the ladies after dinner. It was game night according to the schedule posted, and for once she felt sociable.

Ms. Smith had excused herself to answer the doorbell. Melissa appreciated how nice she had been to her.

"Melissa, can I see you in the office?" Ms. Smith said looking nervous.

"Oh sure, I'll be there in a minute," Melissa answered.

"It's rather urgent," she said wringing her hands.

MELISSA RELUCTANTLY PUSHED THE CAKE PLATE AWAY and got up to follow Ms. Smith.

She was met by a somber looking man in a rather nice suit. Standing next to him was a policewoman.

"Melissa Miller?" the man asked.

"Yes," Melissa answered hesitantly.

"I have a warrant for your arrest for grand theft," he said looking her directly in the face.

Before she could gather her thoughts, a policewoman pulled out handcuffs and put them on her.

Simultaneously, the well-dressed man began speaking.

"Melissa Miller, you have the right to remain silent. Anything you say can and will be used against you in a court of law."

He continued to give the Miranda speech while Melissa stood dazed.

Stunned by the sudden turn of events, Ms. Smith watched Melissa's reaction. She was afraid that this episode would trigger the addiction's power to make her want to zone out.

"I'm sorry, Melissa," Ms. Smith said. "I have no jurisdiction over the Federal Government."

Melissa assumed the well-dressed man must be a detective.

"Can I say something?" she asked.

"I just read you your rights," he said tersely. "If I were you, I'd save it for the judge."

With that remark, he and the female police officer escorted her to the door.

"Just a moment," the policewoman said. "I need to do a standard frisk."

Melissa stood still while the police woman patted her down in a quick but thorough way. Satisfied that there was nothing illegal or detrimental on her, they continued to the car.

"Wait a minute," Ms. Smith said. "The child needs her jacket."

She quickly ran to the bedroom and grabbed the jacket belonging to Melissa from the closet.

She was allowed to put the jacket over her shoulders.

"I'm terribly sorry that it came to this," Ms. Smith said. "I'll pray for you."

Chapter Twenty

THE PASSENGERS DISEMBARKED QUICKLY AND QUIETLY.
The fear of their mishap was still gripping their minds. One lady
was pulling her luggage and shaking her head at the same time.
Instead of going to retrieve their luggage from the baggage claim,
they were escorted to a private room with only their carry-on baggage.

The airport authorities and other men in uniforms were there
to greet them. A gentleman in a uniform representing the airline
walked to the podium after everyone was in the room and seated.

"Ladies and gentlemen," he began slowly and with a voice of
compassion. "Our airline is very sympathetic to your recent experience
on our flight. I understand that some of you are shaken, but thankfully no serious injuries have been reported by the crew. Unfortunately,
the atmosphere is very unstable right now due to weather conditions.
We do our best to monitor and avoid any turbulence when possible,"
he said, removing a handkerchief to wipe his forehead.

"Our staff have placed forms at the table on the right. Please
complete this form and mail it back in the pre-stamped envelope. If
any of your carry-on items were damaged because of the atmospheric
disturbance, the airline would like to know about it. Feel free to take
pictures of your belongings if this occurred," he continued.

"We are grateful for your safe arrival and wish you all the best.
At this time, you are free to get your luggage. We are not aware of
any connecting flights from this part of your journey. If we overlooked
any flights, the gentleman with the red coat can assist you," he said
pointing to his right.

GRACE WAS SEATED NEXT TO PASSENGERS who were in the
front of the plane. As they got up to exit her row, she continued to

sit. She bowed her head and said a silent prayer. The last six hours of her young life were unbelievable. While her prayer was basic and one of thanksgiving, she also asked that something good would come out of her meeting with Mark.

After completing her silent prayer, she raised her head and opened her eyes. Someone was standing in the row in front of her seat. It was Mark.

"I just wanted to thank you again for the ticket," Mark said smiling.

"I'm just glad I was able to help," Grace said.

"You did more than that," he said excitedly. "When I went into the restroom, I had a, a type of encounter," he said. "I don't know how to explain it, but I feel like well ..."

"Renewed?" Grace interjected.

"Yes," he said.

"Some people call it born again," she explained.

Mark's eyes widened. "Well, whatever it's called, I'm grateful," he said.

"I'm happy for you," Grace said. She felt a little guilty because she initially felt like she didn't want to be bothered.

"What do I do next?" he asked sincerely.

"Join a Bible-believing church," she said. "Find one where they love the word of God and teach holy living," she said. "It's time for you to discover the God who has loved you all your life."

She was not sure of what to do next, so she stood up to shake his hand, but he grabbed her and gave her a hug instead. Then he left abruptly. He ignored his friends who were watching from a distance and left the room.

Chapter Twenty-one

"YOU'RE ALLOWED ONE TELEPHONE CALL," the officer said as he escorted Melissa to a cell. "Give some thought to who you need to call, and I will return shortly," he said. Slamming the cell made Melissa shudder. The officer began walking away and then stopped abruptly. "It's none of my business, but I think a nice girl like you ought to be calling her parents," he added. "They must be very worried about you."

Melissa looked down at her hands. There was ink residue from fingerprinting her. She had never been to jail. She looked slowly around the cell and took it all in. So this is what it's like to be in jail, she thought. She had only seen pictures of a cell on television. She didn't feel she was the classiest individual, but she felt the jail was beneath her.

Of course she would call her parents, if that was possible. But it wasn't possible. Her mother was dead. She never knew her real father. She felt railroaded. She felt ashamed. She felt alone.

She was starting to shake a little in her hands. On her third day in rehab, she swore she would never take another prescription drug to get high. But she really felt like she could use a pill. The thought came to her that she was a loser. No one cared about her, except her brother. But she didn't want to bother him. He had escaped the life of abuse and misuse.

She decided it was best to just die and end the horror of her existence. It wouldn't be the first time that she tried to kill herself. She tried it once when she was with a group of friends. They were all depressed and all wanted to escape the pain of their situations. They all took pills and fell asleep. However, she woke up in the hospital.

SHE DROPPED HER HEAD IN ANGUISH and the tears began to flow. "Help me, Lord," she said in a sound just above a whisper. She sat on the stained, sheet-less mattress and buried her face in her hands. Maybe this was just a bad dream and she would wake up any moment now.

The cling clang sound of keys startled her and she raised her head.

The officer who had locked her up moments earlier was opening the cell.

"You're being released, young lady," he said.

Melissa stood suddenly and brushed away the tears streaming down her face. She felt a little strange because she wondered who ordered her release. The police attendant walked her to the desk and signed papers for her dismissal. They returned her jacket and her ring.

As she turned to walk out the door, she saw him and it all made sense. He had paid the bail money. He smiled a gentle, calming smile that seemed to say without words that he didn't judge her. She fell upon his shoulder and wept.

"It's alright, it's alright," Cedric said. "Let's get you home and out of this place," he said. Melissa wanted to explain what had happened. She wanted to tell him more of her story. She wanted to let him know that she really wasn't a bad person. But she couldn't talk. She could only cry and let him console her broken heart.

HE ESCORTED HER TO HIS CAR and took her home. She remembered that her purse and keys and other personal effects were still at the rehab center.

"I can't get in," she said once the car stopped.

"It's ok," Cedric said. He got out the car and opened the trunk. There was a plastic bag with Melissa's purse inside.

"You are the most thoughtful person in the world," she said to him.

"Thanks," he said. "Tomorrow we have to appear in court for an arraignment," he said. "I've taken off work for a few days to help."

"Why do you bother to help me?" Melissa asked. "You have

done more for me than anyone during this ordeal."

"You're a special young lady," Cedric said. "Besides, I don't want you to have a relapse."

He walked her to the door and promised to pick her up the next day. She graciously accepted the invitation and thanked him again for his generosity.

She went directly to the bathroom and turned on the shower. The very memory of the grungy cell made her feel extremely dirty. Once inside the warm beating waters of the flowing jets, she tried to process the kind of day that she had experienced. She thought she was fresh out of tears, but they mingled with the splashing water. I'm trying to turn my life around, she kept telling herself. Why does my life have to be so difficult?

Melissa stayed under the running flow until she had exhausted the supply of hot water. She got out of the shower and deliberated on other matters as she dressed for bed. She knew she should call her brother but was ashamed of where her life had taken her up to this point. Buster was doing great. He had escaped the traps of addiction.

SHE KNEW HER MOTHER WOULD BE PROUD OF BUSTER. But her heart had a heaviness. It was during these times that she would pop a pill to escape the pain of reality. She didn't want to remember her unhappy childhood, and she didn't think she could face an uncertain future. There was always that lurking voice that said what's the use. The voice that said escape forever. She fought the voice that said pop a pill. She did not need to be alone.

She steadied herself and sat on her bed. What was it that the instructor told her? She grabbed her teddy bear from the bed and hugged it tightly as she rocked back and forth. Then she remembered the instructions.

"God loves me," she said out loud. "He loves me in spite of everything. He loves me and he is with me. He loves me and there's nothing anyone can do about it. He loves me and I love him back," she said. Then she crawled into her bed in a fetal position, still holding tightly to her teddy bear. She started over saying the same words. She wasn't sure how long she had said them. But eventually she fell soundly asleep and won the battle.

Chapter Twenty-two

CEDRIC SAT IN RACHEL'S KITCHEN and did his best to comfort his mom.

"What else did they say?" he asked her. Between dealing with the phone call from the rehab center and the phone call from his mother, he wondered if he could be the strong man she needed right now.

"I'm not giving up hope," Rachel said. "That initial call just threw me off my guard."

"Charlie is strong, Mom," Cedric said, trying to console her and convince himself.

"I know that," she said. "It's just hard right now; it's just hard. Do you think God is punishing me?" she asked.

"What? What kind of nonsense are you speaking? Is that the way you view God?" he inquired.

"I just thought that if I were a better person … Maybe if I went to church the way you and Charlie started going. I don't know. I tried to be a good mom. I tried.."

"Mom, the Bible says that God draws us to him with loving kindness. Even the best person in the world has to deal with the circumstances of life. Sometimes that's good and sometimes it's bad. Remember the story of Job?" he said.

Rachel nodded her head in agreement.

"Job lived an outstanding life. He still had people who accused him of doing something in private. But he knew that he loved God and was faithful."

"That's what scares me, Cedric," she said. "I know I'm not perfect. I always tried to do right by you boys and now this," she said grabbing a tissue from the table. "I tried to be a good employee. I try to do right by the neighbors and I go to church every now and then," she said.

"Mom, those things are really great," Cedric said. Remember when I was in the hospital with pneumonia when I was eleven?" he asked. "I remember the hospital chaplain coming by to pray with you and me. I heard you promise God to give him your life," he said.

"Yeah, I know," she admitted. "I think I really did become a better person," Rachel explained.

"Mom," Cedric said lovingly. "God is not looking for you to be a better person outside of him. He wants a relationship with you. He loves you with an everlasting love. When we were in camp many years ago, the counselor was able to help me to understand that God is a loving father. That was difficult for me at first, since my father was not a part of my life. I used to think it was because I was imperfect in some way or that God let him die early because he didn't care about me."

Rachel wept when he said those words. "I had no idea," she said. "I'm sorry you felt that way."

"Mom, it's alright now," Cedric said. "I now know that my image of God shouldn't be based on the imperfections of man. After all, God thought I was worth dying for, and when he hung on that cross, I know that he saw me."

"Do you think it's too late for me to have a real relationship with God?" Rachel asked her son sincerely.

"Not according to the Bible," Cedric responded. "As a matter of fact, I don't believe God orchestrated the disappearance of my brother, but he's so good that he can turn any situation around that was meant for bad. On Sunday our guest minister preached about Romans 8:28. And we know that all things work together for good to those who love God, to those who are the called according to His purpose."

Rachel squeezed his hand. "Would you pray for me, son?" she asked.

Cedric got teary eyed. He had wanted his mother to know the Lord for years now. She had always put him off with one excuse after another. While she was happy that he and Charlie loved to go to the youth mission and Christian events, she never really understood their enthusiasm and passion. She considered herself a Christian but had never had any real experiences with God. All of that was about to change.

Cedric wasted no time. "Mom," he said, "I'm going to pray a simple prayer. While I pray, I want you to see in your mind's eye Jesus hanging on the cross. I want you to see him hanging and thinking of you."

"Father, in Jesus name," he began. "My mother wants to know you in a real way. She wants to know you as Savior and Lord," he said. "Mom, repeat after me," he said quietly.

"Dear Jesus, I acknowledge you as the only God. I repent of my sins and ask that you cleanse me from all unrighteousness. I ask you to be Lord of my life and take me to heaven to live with you."

Rachel repeated the prayer with closed eyes and a bowed head. Somehow when she finished, her heart was lighter.

"Can I add a prayer to this one?" she asked.

Cedric nodded his head.

"Dear Lord, I don't know where my son is. I don't know his condition or if he's even alive. I just ask that you allow us to bring him home. If he is alive, I ask that you keep him alive until he's found," she said. "Amen."

"Amen," Cedric said and hugged his mother tighter than he ever had before.

Chapter Twenty-three

LIEUTENANT HUTSON VOLUNTEERED to be a part of the dual mission. The squadron was assigned to search and rescue along with reconnaissance. He considered Charlie a respectable soldier as well as a friend. They had not known each other very long, but he definitely knew there was something special about that young man. There was something to be admired. He knew how to get the soldiers to listen attentively. He also knew how to get them to follow orders and like it.

The desert was a difficult place to chart, and the temperature was never kind. The soldiers were airlifted by helicopter to the area that led to where the little girl in the marketplace said she had been given the dog tags. The place seemed unchartered as they went through the crags and cliffs and finally found real pathways that led to where the village was located.

The rest of the journey would have to be by foot as they searched through mountainous terrain. They were grateful for the villager who agreed to be paid to take them there. He wanted to take them the entire way by foot, but the army insisted on flying to redeem the time. Once they were out of the choppers, he seemed unbothered by the climbing or the heat that beat down upon them. Before long there was a clearing, and then a small village appeared.

LIEUTENANT HUTSON LOOKED AMAZED that people could live in a remote village as if the rest of the world didn't matter. When he thought hard about it, he realized that to these people their world was where they lived. They would come down to the regional market to trade often enough, but they had no hopes of discovering what awaited them beyond their war-torn country. Modest was one way to describe the dwelling places of these families. But simple was a better choice. Lieutenant Hutson kept his eyes sharp and his finger close to the trigger of the army rifle that he carried. While most of the villagers smiled when they saw his squadron, you never knew what was on the minds of the Afghan people. The tour guide stopped one of the villagers that was herding a group of goats. "Abdul," he said to the man and continued speaking in their native language. They conversed momentarily, and the man pointed to a place that appeared to be higher in the mountain.

The guide continued walking and gestured for the soldiers to follow him. They walked about ten minutes and were on the outskirts of the village. It was time to climb higher to the elevation that would prove challenging to the soldiers. Lieutenant Hutson told the men to stand guard and he would go higher with the guide.

Strangely he was led up a bit higher and then down a path that put them back on normal ground. Lieutenant Hutson noticed that to get to this location you needed to follow specific directions or you would miss the opening. It could easily be a secret hideout.

Someone was cooking over an open flame. It seemed odd because it was so hot outside. It was like an American barbecue setting without the meat. The old man attending to the pot used a stick to bring up white rags. Lieutenant Hutson was baffled. These people were poor, but why would they boil rags.

His guide approached a man and they talked in a serious tone. The guide pointed to his own neck and back at Lieutenant Hutson. He then reluctantly took him inside a cavernous home. Lieutenant Hutson looked carefully around, then followed.

His height was much taller than the carved opening allowed. He bent low and looked around the home. It took a moment for his eyes to adjust to the darkness. He then let his attention follow the glowing of an oil lamp. Makeshift beds were in the room. His guide was in the corner looking down on someone wrapped in tattered pieces of cloth from head to toe. Lieutenant Hutson went closer to the injured mummy-looking person. He gasped and nearly fainted. The man was laying on his left side, and the glow seemed to capture the area of his right shoulder where it barely revealed the engraving of a tattoo. One that was shaped like a heart with a cupid's arrow going through it.

Chapter Twenty-four

"CAROL OF THE BELLS" was playing softly in the background. Buster had just returned from a wreck that left two people hospitalized and two small children with minor injuries. He showered and prayed a prayer of thanksgiving. He made a habit of doing this whenever he returned from an emergency call. Now it appeared he had a few minutes to make a call. He anxiously dialed the number and waited for her to pick up.

"Hello, sweetheart," he said.

Her heart leaped to hear his voice. "Buster," she said almost in a whisper. "I've got so much to tell you. I feel like I've been gone forever, and I met this guy on the plane and the plane nearly crashed …"

"Whoa!" Buster responded. "What are you talking about? What happened with your plane? And what do you mean, you met a guy?"

"Ok," Grace said trying to compose her thoughts and herself. "It's kind of a long story," she said. "Can we meet for lunch?" she said with hopeful anticipation.

"Sorry, babe, I'm still on duty and I've got to take an emergency trip to see Melissa," he explained.

"What happened to Melissa?" Grace asked.

"It's another long story that I don't have all the answers to yet. But first tell me about this emergency situation on your plane," he said.

"Well," Grace began, "I thought I would have this nice, quiet flight since it was a red eye," she said. "Then there's this guy that sat next to me," she said trying to organize everything that had happened.

"But Grace," Buster said, "tell me about the plane and then get back to the guy. I want to know that you're ok!"

"Sweetheart, you endure so much drama through your day that I really don't want to scare you with what could have happened," she said.

"I signed up to know what could have happened to the person I intend to spend the rest of my life with," he said in a caring tone.

"That's why I love you so much," she said with tears. "You not only care about me, but you care about what could have happened to me," she said. "It was the weather that caused all the commotion," she explained. "We were sort of taken off guard. We lost altitude without warning and people were very shaken and items were thrown around. It was quite scary. I tried to do my best to stay calm, but all I could think about was you."

"You thought about me instead of your parents?" he said. "You must really like me a lot!" he joked.

"Cut it out, Bernard!" she said loudly.

"Uh oh, you're using my first name. I'll behave. What happened next?"

"Well, as I was saying, I thought about you and how you had led me to Christ. I was sort of afraid but not to the point of panic," she said with great emotion. "I knew in my heart that I would be alright," she said.

For a moment there was silence on the other end. "Are you still there, Buster?" she asked.

"I'm here. I'm so sorry that I wasn't there to protect you," he said.

"Buster, I know you save people every day from disasters and accidents. But sweetheart, you're not Superman. I mean you're my Superman, but you can't keep airplanes from falling or keep cars from wrecking or things like that. I'm just thrilled that at the end of the day, I get to tell you how Jesus protected me and kept me safe," she said.

"Sounds like an unbelievable experience," he said.

"Oh, it was. The captain and the airline people put us all in a room afterward to make sure we were ok. I think they are going to offer us some compensation for our miserable trip," she said.

"Oh good, maybe we can use it for our honeymoon," he said. They both laughed, and Buster realized in his heart that they were blessed to have one another.

"Now tell me about Melissa," Grace said.

"Well she's in some sort of trouble, and I need to figure out what's going on with her," he said. "I'm driving down the day after tomorrow, since I have the next five days off."

"I hope the weather is ok," Grace said.

"Hey, wait a minute," Buster said changing the subject before Grace could start worrying about his driving situation. "You wanted to tell me something about a guy you met on the plane," he said.

"Oh yes, you see while I was waiting for the last..."

Just as she began her story, the fireman's alarm sounded and Buster gave a quick goodbye and hung up the phone.

Grace was used to it. As a nurse, she knew every second mattered when lives were at stake.

Chapter Twenty-five

RACHEL ATTENDED CHURCH with Cedric on Sunday. It felt so good to know she was now a part of the community of believers. She sat in the service thinking about her preconceived ideas of being a Christian and how they had been totally wrong. Her basic ideas had been formed by television, other people and her own opinions. She never understood the concept of reading God's word and believing it to be infallible. But now sitting in the atmosphere of worshippers, she knew she was in the right place but had a lot to learn. She met the young pastor before service and told him that she planned to join the congregation officially on the next Sunday.

Cedric promised to take his mother to look at Christmas trees after service. It would certainly keep her mind clear of worrying about Charlie. Rachel loved Christmas, and if anything could help her stay distracted, it would be the holiday spirit.

He knew of a large nursery near his apartment that probably had every tree imaginable. Of course, his mom's favorite tree would be the Blue Spruce. He would be happy to purchase it for her and she could decorate it all day Monday if she liked. He would be in court with Melissa. She had asked for some time alone to gather her thoughts. He respected the fact that she didn't make any special requests of him. He liked her and wanted to show her the love of God.

"Cedric," his mother whispered to get his attention. "Please pass the offering plate," she said.

Cedric's mind was so busy wandering that he didn't realize it was offering time. He heard someone making announcements and his mind just drifted off.

"Honey, I know you're worried about your brother," Rachel whispered.

"That's part of it, and I was also thinking about Melissa," he said.

"When are you going to bring her to see me? I thought she would have called me by now," Rachel said.

"We'll discuss it after church," Cedric said. He then focused on the service as the choir began to sing a very uplifting song. He tried to stay focused in case his mother had any questions about the service.

CEDRIC NOTICED A TEAR roll down the face of his mother while the choir was singing "How Great is Our God." It was one of his favorites. He became weepy himself as he realized the dream of having his mother sit beside him in an atmosphere of worship.

The pastor immediately took the microphone after the choir completed their song. He took the mic quickly and began talking as if he was in a hurry.

"Does anybody in here want to go to heaven? I said is there anybody in here who wants to go to heaven?" he repeated as if he was limited to only a few minutes. "Why am I talking about heaven? I'm glad you asked," he said walking back and forth on the stage. "You see I had intended to talk to you today about the 23rd Psalm. I intended to talk to you about goodness and mercy and still waters. I wanted to speak sweetly to you about your enemies having to watch you enjoy the blessings of God. But I had a dream last night. I said I had a dream last night. In this dream I was told to warn the people to get ready," he said with conviction. "You already know the 23rd Psalm. You know about the shepherd and his sheep. But I want to know if you know where you will spend eternity!" he said with his eyes widening. Do you have your ticket to heaven?" he asked.

CEDRIC FELT CHILL BUMPS when he asked that question.

"Don't you know the fare has already been paid? Have you been washed in the blood of the Lamb? Have you been filled with the Spirit of God? Oh, I know," the pastor said. "You thought today, you'd come to church, stay 30 minutes, then leave after fulfilling your obligatory duty. Well after I fell asleep last night, I saw some things that I have never seen before. Things you are not able to bear. But I just want to warn men and women, boys and girls to get ready. Jesus is coming! I said Jesus is coming!" he said with tears in his eyes. "Are you ready, church? Is your house in order? Are you expecting him the way a pregnant mother expects to deliver a child? Each month the time draws closer. Then you'll hear her say, 'Any day now, I will deliver,'" he said.

"Lord, forgive me for watching the stock market more than looking for your return," he said. "I'm sorry that I invested more in my career than I invested in your leadership. Help me to warn these little ones that time is so short and that your return is near. Help me to convince them not to be left behind or to try to survive in the world system," he said with his head bowed and tears flowing down his cheeks.

Rachel wasn't sure what to do. She felt in her soul every passionate word he was saying.

"Now I don't want to fail to mention that Heaven doesn't really exist without hell. We will all stand before God one day covered with excuses or covered by the blood of Jesus. Only one is acceptable. Which one will you have? Revelations 20:12 says the books were opened. One day God will open the books and we each will have one chapter," he said holding his Bible up above his head. "It will be animated and reveal everything we've done in these bodies. I wish he were looking for good deeds. I wish he was looking for status. I wish he was looking for good people, but he's looking for one thing. He's looking for the blood of his Holy son Jesus."

He asked the congregation to reference Psalm 19:14.

"Repeat after me," he said. "Let the words of my mouth, and the meditation of my heart, be acceptable in thy sight, O Lord my strength, and my redeemer."

Afterward, he offered prayer for anyone desiring salvation or experiencing problems. He invited them to come to the front of the church. He told them to come quickly! Rachel watched people come from each direction, then she quickly got up and joined them. She felt whatever the preacher was feeling, and somehow she was not ashamed. he wanted the passion that he was delivering in his message.

The pastor put his hand on her shoulder and prayed that God would work a miracle on her behalf. She wiped the tears and returned to her seat. She wondered how the pastor knew that she needed a miracle.

After the service, Rachel spoke with Cedric about her experience.

"Cedric, did you tell the pastor that Charlie was missing in action?" she asked.

"No, I could never reach him," he said.

"He prayed that I would receive a miracle," she stressed.

"Oh, that sounds like discernment of the Holy Spirit," he answered.

"Cedric, I felt something electrifying as he spoke," Rachel said. "It wasn't fear either. It was a longing to be with God. I want to be right in my heart. I want to know that when I die, I will spend eternity with God and with my children," she said. "Thank you for bringing me here today. I will continue to hold on to my faith and believe God for a miracle for my son, my dear son. I want to go home and check for messages," she said. "Sorry about your plans for the Christmas tree. I don't want to decorate a tree unless I know that Charlie is safe."

Chapter Twenty-six

BUSTER WAS GRATEFUL that there was no snow to contend with as he left the city. But he hadn't counted on the fog. He explained to Grace that his sister was in some sort of trouble. He purposely didn't tell her that he always had trouble on this date. He never liked to be around people when this time of the year rolled around. It was the anniversary of his mother's death.

It had been a few years since she passed, but Buster was always emotional during this time. He always wondered why the good died young. He saw it often in his line of work. Innocent children were often the victims of some freak accident.

In his rush to visit Melissa and clear his mind, Buster tried to focus on good thoughts. He decided to think about Grace and what she meant to him. But when he thought of her, he wished he could have introduced her to his mother. He thought about his career as a firefighter. But his focus drifted to being named the rookie firefighter of the year two years ago and his mom missing such an important occasion.

He remembered all the good times spent with her. Their family wasn't perfect and didn't pretend to be perfect. Yet he knew his mom tried to raise them the best she could. He remembered that he and Melissa were traumatized on that dreadful day when Stan the Ice Cream Man was killed. He remembered the countless nightmares of wondering why this awful thing had happened. Ms. Rachel had accepted counseling for her boys from the free clinic. He wished he and Melissa had been able to do that. But his mom's boyfriend Marvin never took them while his mom worked. He was too busy drinking or smoking that stinky marijuana.

There were so many memories that he really wanted to forget.

He wished to God that he could hide them in a corner of his mind and lock the door on them. But there was something about anniversaries. They came every year, and when they came he had to find a way to cope with a part of his life that was unpleasant and unforgettable. He knew when he accepted Christ that things had improved a whole lot. He also knew that God was with him and helping him to take life one day at a time. He was grateful. He just needed to process his experiences little by little to get through this unforgettable day marking the tragic death of his mom.

Buster's first mistake was driving too fast while he dealt with his thoughts. His second mistake was tailgating so that he could get past the Brooklyn Bridge. Having left very early in the morning, his intent was to get ahead of the morning commuters. However, in New York City there is always continual and unexpected traffic.

His speed was within the limits of the law. But everybody knows that when there is fog, you must stay under the speed limit and try to keep a safe driving distance. Buster was thinking about his sister and his childhood, driving and drinking coffee. The thick fog was so annoying that he decided to use two hands and put the coffee down. He had just cleared the bridge when he looked briefly for his cup holder.

Visibility was less than three car lengths ahead. After clearing the bridge, there were two ways that he could go. Buster noticed a neon sign giving specific directions to turn with the symbol for turn right. There was too much on his mind. For a moment he became confused regarding left and right. Buster wasn't sure where the motorcyclist came from, but he jumped in front of Buster, which caused him to veer off to the right and take that direction to avoid hitting him. He didn't get a good look at the man except for the fact that he had a long torso and it was a huge bike; maybe a Harley. Now Buster was forced to take this direction out of town because there was no turning back in the thick fog. This direction would be slower, but he had no choice.

Seconds after veering right, he heard loud screeching and the sound of cars smashing into one another. He had just missed that, whatever it was. He was grateful to God for not being in the pileup. He needed to get to his sister. He thought of calling Grace to talk to her while he navigated through the fog and made his way to Interstate 80.

GRACE WAS SUCH A GODSEND TO HIM. She was pretty and smart, and he was blessed to introduce her to the Lord. He knew she was the one for him from the first time he met her in the elevator. That's why he gave her his precious ticket to heaven. He knew that she carried it with her and treasured it. After their marriage, it would again be part of his life and they would share all that it meant to them both. He was thinking that they should put it in their family Bible. He was so grateful that she was in his life. It was great to have someone to share his life experiences with. There was so much drama in his profession. He was looking forward to coming home from work someday soon after their marriage to just spend time with the love of his life.

Chapter Twenty-seven

MELISSA ARRIVED AT THE COURTHOUSE EARLY. She wasn't sure if she needed a lawyer or what was about to take place. She paced back and forth in front of the court's entry. Her biggest question to herself was how did she get here. She had tried to kill herself on two occasions. Each time she tried, she had failed. She couldn't really put into words how she felt about her life. She felt lost on many days and hopeless on others. Everything went sour when her mother died. How did people survive the loss of someone so important in their lives?

She wondered what it would be like to have a normal life. Someone her age should be coming out of college and stepping into a new venture in life. She had dreams too! She wanted a real family of her own. One where there was no abuse, no neglect and no secrets. It looked like things were improving as she had discussions in the center with other women with similar experiences. They made a pact to all do better and be accountable to someone. Then it seemed she was just pulled off that highway of deliverance. Dear God, she said in her heart, am I just worthless?

Melissa heard footsteps and looked behind her. It was just the morning custodian putting fresh trash bags in the hallway cans. She continued pacing while looking down at her shoes. They were black penny loafers, and she wore them with all of her slacks on important occasions. Today was one of those occasions. She was still looking down when someone tapped her on the shoulder. As a natural reaction, she spun around quickly and found a caring face. It was Cedric. She quickly hugged him and said, "Thanks for coming."

"What else have I got to do?" he said smiling.

"Cedric, I don't know what to say. Do I need a lawyer? What will I tell Buster? He has no idea what's going on now. Do you think I should call him? Can you believe what's happening to me?" she said in about a breath and a half.

"Maybe, I don't know, maybe and maybe," he said answering the questions in order with what she considered to be an annoying smile.

"I'm sorry," she said. "I had too much coffee this morning."

"I do have one word of advice," Cedric said looking her directly in the eye. "Just tell the truth," he said. "Things always go better in the end when you tell the truth."

Cedric reached in his jacket pocket and pulled out an envelope. "My mom and I are dealing with a crisis right now," he said. "My brother Charlie is missing in Iraq," he said looking her directly in the eye.

"Charlie?" she said. "I'm so sorry. You guys were so much like our family growing up. Oh, I hope they find him," she said squeezing Cedric's hand.

Cedric opened the envelope that he held and handed her the contents. "This is something very special to me that I think you could use today," he said. "You were probably too young to remember Stan the Ice Cream Man," he said.

"As a matter of fact, I do remember," she said. "I still have the ring that he gave me that day. I could never seem to lose it or get rid of it. I still treasure it, but I won't wear it because the nightmares might start up again," she said.

"Wow," said Cedric. "You were probably four or five and that day is engraved in your mind too. I will try to be here as long as I can, but I might have to leave early if it takes longer than a few hours," he said. "I've got to complete some things at work."

A GUARD WITH JINGLING KEYS began to open the door to the courtroom. Melissa and Cedric stood watching and waited for him to complete the process. Then they followed him inside.

108

She had thirty minutes left before she was scheduled to appear. She and Cedric chose to sit on the left side in the third row. Just as they sat down, Cedric's phone rang. He told her he would take it outside.

That gave Melissa some privacy as she read the contents of the envelope. She noticed that the document said Ticket to Heaven. Her curiosity was piqued, and she engrossed herself in reading the document. When she finally looked up there were at least 10 other people in different areas of the courtroom. Cedric had not returned. Moments later a bailiff announced the entrance of the judge.

"All rise," the bailiff declared while giving the formal introduction of the judge. Melissa didn't hear the name because her nerves were wearing thin. She closed her eyes and waited for the instruction to take her seat.

"The People of Northern Pharmacy vs. Melissa Miller," the bailiff announced.

"Proceed," the judge said after telling the audience to be seated.

A middle-aged man wearing a solid blue suit with a red tie stood and began reading charges that were targeted at Melissa.

"Your honor, Melissa Miller is a 23-year-old woman who was hired eighteen months ago to work as a technical pharmacy stocker. Six months ago, she and three other workers were fired after a continual discrepancy in the count of some controlled pharmaceuticals. An investigation ensued in which it was discovered that five thousand dollars suddenly appeared in said plaintiff's account. The FBI was called to investigate, and the evidence is inconclusive at this time. The pharmaceutical company believes the drugs were sold and the money was put into the account. Ms. Miller suddenly left the area and was tracked to this city in a rehabilitation facility."

"If the evidence was inconclusive, why was she charged?" the judge asked.

"Agent Wallace Yarbrough from the FBI is present and can answer that question."

AGENT YARBROUGH CAME TO THE FRONT of the judge's seat and began talking.

"Your honor, Melissa Miller was booked on suspicion of carrying contraband across state lines. By law, we can hold her for 24 hours for questioning in such cases," he said.

Melissa was afraid and kept reading and rereading the card that Cedric had given her. You are loved by God, the ticket read. Nothing can separate you from the love of God.

"Is the plaintiff or defendant present?" the judge asked.

"Melissa Miller is the accused and she is present," the bailiff said.

"Have the accused approach," the judge said.

"Melissa Miller, please approach the bench," the judge said.

Melissa walked to the front trying to steady her nerves.

"Young lady, are you aware of what you're being accused of?" the judge said.

"I am, your honor," Melissa answered nervously.

The judge flipped through the file in front of him, looked at Melissa and reread the file.

"Are you or have you ever been a user of narcotics?" the judge asked.

Melissa remembered the advice Cedric had given her. "I was addicted to certain narcotics until recently," Melissa said. "However, I had nothing to do with the medication missing from the pharmacy," Melissa added.

"How did you maintain your drug habit?" the judge asked. "Unless you had a secret fund to supply your habit, I need to know where you got your drugs and money from," he said sternly.

"Your honor, my narcotics were obtained legally. Due to an issue, a traumatic issue," she repeated, trying to steady her nerves, "that I witnessed as a child, the drugs were written to help me cope with my nightmares. I continued to fill the prescription under a doctor's care. I know now that the doctor should not have been so accommodating," she said.

"Do you have proof of this doctor's existence and records to show your prescription?"

"Yes sir, I do," she said.

"What about this mysterious appearance of," he paused to look at her paperwork filed, "5,000 dollars in your account?" he said.

"My mother died of cancer, your honor, about 10 years ago. Her insurance policy left me and my brother $5,000 each upon turning a certain age," she said. "That happened just recently," she said. "I was in an abusive relationship when I got the news from the insurance company," she continued. "I left town suddenly and opened an account for the money just a few days ago," she explained.

"When I received word that the money would be released, I wanted to come back to this city with the high hope of starting over and breaking my dependency on prescription drugs," she said.

"Is there anyone here to validate your story?" the judge asked.

Melissa shook her head and said, "Unfortunately, your honor ..."

"The validator is late," Cedric said finishing her sentence. My name is Cedric Grimes, and I've known Melissa since she was a little girl. Her mother did indeed pass away from cancer. I work at the bank where Melissa made the deposit. I personally opened up the account that Melissa wanted to deposit her insurance money."

The judge did a double take when Cedric appeared. Then he did a quick smile.

Melissa clung to the ticket to heaven and read the final paragraph.

This ticket is also good for navigating through life on earth. Your journey will be unique. You will have hard times, good times, strange times and stressful times. But if you wholeheartedly embrace the one this ticket represents, you will make it through every time. Jesus Christ backs this ticket and with him all things are possible. Memorize his words that are included in this ticket. Stamp them in your heart. For he has declared "I will never leave you or forsake you."

"Mr. Cedric Grimes is a fine, outstanding citizen," the judge said. "I'm releasing Melissa on his word and throwing out the case," he said hitting his gavel on the desk.

Cedric then realized that the judge was the customer at his bank that he helped to find the right key for the safe deposit box. He smiled and escorted Melissa back to her seat.

"All rise," the bailiff said loudly. The judge stood and returned through the back door where he had appeared.

Cedric gave Melissa a big hug and escorted her out of the courtroom.

"Thank you, Lord," he whispered softly. He noticed that Melissa was wiping away a tear. The courtroom hallway now had music playing very softly. The choir was singing 'Joy to the World the Lord is Come.'

Chapter Twenty-eight

LIEUTENANT HUTSON USED HIS RADIO communication to alert his superiors that Charlie had been found. It was an arduous mission because of his remote location. His fellow soldiers let out a cheer when they got the news and began hugging one another. They had no idea of what condition he was in, but they heard that he was alive. To them, that was all that mattered.

Lieutenant Hutson hung with his buddy the entire distance. He was first airlifted to the Combat Support Hospital. The CSH was on the base and awaiting his arrival for assessment. Lieutenant Hutson kept speaking to Charlie but there was no response. It was not evident what part of him needed immediate attention. There were lots of scrapes and bruises and sores. He suspected there was internal trauma.

News of his discovery exploded on the base like a bomb. Major Butler was in the office when all officers were summoned to the general's office.

"What's going on, Chaplain Bartley?" Major Butler asked.

"I'm about to find out," he said. "Just before rushing out the door, he turned to her and said, "Say a prayer for Charlie. I've got a feeling that this is about him."

Major Butler put both her hands to her face to cover the emotion that was rushing into her body. She wasn't sure if this was good news or bad, but she had a feeling she would know soon enough.

Chaplain Bartley hopped in his jeep to drive to the office. He could have walked but did not want to delay the news. He passed the sober-faced General Galster walking on his way there. He did not offer him a ride. He was too anxious to hear the news.

THE ROOM QUICKLY FILLED with those in top command. The generals took their seats and waited for the news of what was coming down the pike. Chaplain Bartley sat where he could look out the window toward the mountains. Psalm 121 immediately came to his mind. He dropped his head and said a silent prayer.

After the arrival of General Galster, Lieutenant General Lincoln began to speak. As communications general, it was his responsibility to relay any messages from the field to the commanding officers.

"Gentlemen, at 1600 hours it was discovered that Captain Charlie Grimes was in a remote mountainous location. The recent discovery of his military identification tag by Lieutenant Hutson through some local Iraqi people led to the finding of the soldier in a small village in a remote mountain. Our medical team is on standby to receive the soldier, who will be airlifted here by helicopter momentarily. So far the only assessment of his condition is that he is alive," said Lieutenant General Lincoln.

The eruption of enthusiasm was spontaneous among the high-ranking officials. There was applause and high fives through-out the table. The only sober looking person was General Galster. He managed an acceptable smile, although from Chaplain Bartley's position, it appeared disingenuous.

"We will certainly interview Lieutenant Hutson and--" he began. A sudden sound in the distance invaded the room and grew louder. One of the generals recognized it as a helicopter. The generals all wanted to run to the window like school boys anxious to get to a playground. They, however, were high ranking officers and that behavior was not tolerated.

Shortly after the helicopter's landing, the meeting was adjourned until further notice. Chaplain Bartley used his jeep to get to the medical facility as fast as he could. While the other officers would surely be turned away, he had an obligation to ensure that all soldiers had access to someone that could provide spiritual direction and prayer.

To the surprise of Chaplain Bartley, Major Butler was already in the waiting room. He threw his head back and laughed. "There's a leak somewhere in our top-secret alliance," he said.

She ignored his remark and spoke of the real issue at hand. "I didn't get here in time to see him," she said. "I did ask the attendant and found ..."

"Chaplain Bartley?" the doctor interrupted after stepping into the waiting area. "I'd like to see you in the backroom, sir."

Chaplain Bartley excused himself and followed the doctor to a small room not much larger than a closet.

"I'm still doing some testing, but my initial examination is that Captain Grimes is in a coma possibly caused by a severe concussion. There is some reaction like blinking when I look at his pupils," the doctor said soberly.

"I'll be praying for him," Chaplain Bartley said.

"That's wonderful, Chaplain, but that's not why I called you here. His family needs to be told and someone needs to accompany him to Landstahl, Germany for treatment. Unfortunately, I can't spare any hospital personnel at this time. Can you make a recommendation to the commanding General?"

"With the General's permission, I'll make the call to his family," the Chaplain said courageously. "I'm sure I have a recommendation for his traveling companion as well."

"Thank you, sir," the physician said while opening the door to quickly get back to the patient.

Chaplain Bartley offered a ride to Major Butler, but she refused and asked permission to stay until she could see Charlie in person.

After granting the permission, Chaplain Bartley went to the commanding general to make his recommendation. He had seen a lot of injuries during his tenure as a chaplain. He was grateful that Charlie had returned with all his limbs. His prayer was that he would wake from the coma having all of his faculties.

HE MADE HIS WAY to the commanding general's office. He was relieved that he didn't have to deal with General Galster. He would speak directly with General McMiller. Whenever he was on the base, he was in charge. That didn't happen very often, but he was present this week.

Upon entering his office, he saluted the five-star general.

"At ease, Chaplain. I've been expecting you. I just got off the phone with the doctor. I understand that you've volunteered to contact the family. That's good news," General McMiller said.

"I also have a recommendation," Chaplain Bartley said quickly. "I believe Lieutenant Hutson would be a great companion to escort Captain Grimes," Chaplain Bartley said.

"I agree," General McMiller said. "Especially since he worked so closely with him and singlehandedly found him," he said. "Unfortunately, I can't spare him right now."

"Sir?" Chaplain Bartley said, looking a bit dazed.

"You heard me right, Chaplain. There's another mission coming up soon and I need the men to train for it. The excellent work by Lieutenant Hutson just won him a chance to lead the squadron. Any other recommendations?"

"As a matter of fact, I do have one more recommendation, General," Chaplain Bartley said. "It may seem a bit unconventional."

Chapter Twenty-nine

BUSTER ARRIVED SAFE AND SOUND into the city. He was very anxious to see his sister and very grateful to be alive. He heard on the radio that someone was critically injured in the pileup just off the Brooklyn Bridge. Good thing the motorcyclist caused me to veer to the right, he thought.

He wanted to go see his aunt, but he didn't want the drama attached to it. He also didn't want to drive another five hours. Instead, he decided to go directly to the address Melissa had given him a month earlier.

Melissa felt a weight had been lifted off her shoulders after the court appearance. She was so glad she had told the truth. She also made it a point to say a prayer that night. She kept rereading the ticket that Cedric had given her. She didn't know how to explain it, but she knew that it was very valuable.

She had enough energy to do laundry. She picked up the basket to go to the common laundry facility beneath her apartment. She opened the door and dropped the basket. There stood her big brother with a huge grin on his face.

"Perfect timing," he said. "Hello, Lissa."

Melissa put out one arm to hug him and the other hand over her mouth to hold back the emotion that would have come out in an alarming fashion.

"It's ok, it's ok," he told her. "Everything is gonna be alright," he said as he wrapped his arms around this little girl that he had tried to protect all his life. Melissa wept quietly and stained her brother's shirt with her tears.

"I hate to break this up," he said," but I'd love to come inside and relax a bit. I've been on the road for hours you know."

"Sorry, Buster," she said. "I was just so shocked to see you. Why didn't you tell me you were coming?" she said, opening the door to let him in.

"I guess I wanted to surprise you," he said.

"Well, it really worked. You want something to drink?" she offered.

"You got any coffee?" he asked.

"No, all I have is tea and I know you don't like tea. Hey, I'm supposed to have lunch with a friend in about 45 minutes. I'll call him and tell him that I have a ride. I want you to meet this person. It's a surprise, so don't ask questions, ok? Just relax for about 60 minutes and then we will leave. Ok?"

"Ok, lil sis," he said as he put his head gently back on her couch to take a nap.

BUSTER'S HEAD HAD BARELY TOUCHED THE SOFT MATERIAL before he was clearly out. Melissa took that time to alert Cedric that she would be there shortly. She felt special. That was something she hadn't allowed herself to feel in a long time. She could remember feeling lonely and remember feeling hopeless, but for the first time in many years she actually felt special.

She freshened up and made sure the ticket was in her purse before waking Buster. He was groggy, but he would do whatever he could to make his little sister happy.

He was pleased to know the restaurant was only 10 minutes away. When they arrived, they asked for a table so that they could quickly be served. Melissa was on the lookout for Cedric, while Buster perused the menu.

The minute she saw him enter the restaurant, she waved him over to the table. Buster's back was to Cedric as he walked over to them. Buster put the menu down and looked up. There staring at him was his childhood friend. Buster jumped up and grabbed his old friend, grinning from ear to ear. He had no idea he would see

Cedric today. Both were clueless in the reunion of sorts. The happiness went on for a brief moment. It concluded when Buster asked about Charlie.

Cedric sat down and a veil of uneasiness took over his face. We found out this week that he's missing in action," he said almost in a whisper. The shock on Buster's face included embarrassment for casually asking such a sensitive question.

"He's been in Iraq for a number of months," Cedric said. "Mom and I are keeping the faith. They've been actively looking for him since his squadron was rescued recently. The army is so secretive. They promised to contact us as soon as there is more news," Cedric continued.

"So how did you find Melissa?" Buster asked.

"I believe everything happens for a reason," Cedric said. "Melissa came walking into my bank. I work there; I don't own it," he clarified. "She came inside to open an account. I hardly recognized her," he said. "She's grown up to be such a beautiful, young woman," Cedric remarked. "She was giving me some vital information when I looked up and noticed her dimple," he said smiling. "I've only known one person to have that dimple, and it was a cute little girl named Lissa," he said. "What have you been up to, Buster?"

"I live in New York, well Manhattan specifically," Buster said. "I'm a firefighter for the city. I love saving lives," he said. "As a matter of fact, that's how I met my fiancé."

"Fiancé? Well congratulations, Buster," Cedric said with a slapped handshake.

"Her name is Grace, and she is definitely good news worth spreading. Which reminds me of the accident we all lived through when we were kids," Buster said.

"You mean the one with Stan the Ice Cream Man?" Cedric asked.

"You better believe it," Buster said. "And guess what? I still have my ticket, well sort of. I gave it to my fiancé, so technically I still have it."

"Me too," Cedric said. "Well, technically I loaned it to a good friend of mine," he said giving a quick wink to Melissa. "You know," Cedric said with a pondering look on his face, "there's one thing that bothers me still to this day."

"What's that?" Melissa asked.

"The day of the accident, Mr. Stan said the tickets he was giving us were for his children. I remember that remark like it was yesterday. I know this is going to sound crazy," Cedric said, "but what if we had the opportunity to find them?"

"Are you ready to order?" the waitress said standing in front of them. She seemed in a hurry, so they all ordered burgers and fries and colas.

"I'll be back shortly," she said smiling the smile of a tired worker.

"Find who?" Buster said continuing their conversation.

"Find his children and give them the tickets," Cedric said enthusiastically.

"Oh, but they would be grown by now and well," Melissa said groping for an excuse.

"It's the holiday season," Cedric said. "Can you imagine how getting a 20-year-old gift from your late dad could make a person feel?"

"But we don't know anything about his kids, or where they are or anything," Buster explained.

"I know," Cedric said. "But I always had this detective side of me for figuring things out. I guess that's how I got into banking. I solve money problems. Let me do some research and see what I can find out. Then we'll get our tickets and present them to the kids if they want them," he said.

"It could be the worst thing we've ever done or the best thing we've ever done," Buster said. "But I'm in town for a few days, so let's try it," he said.

Melissa took her cool drink from the waitress and began drinking it. She felt chill bumps, but it wasn't from the ice cold drink.

Chapter Thirty

TEARS WERE RUNNING DOWN RACHEL'S FACE as she hung up the telephone. She fell to her knees sobbing. God had answered her prayer.

"Charlie's alive, he's alive," she kept saying as she repeated the words that Chaplain Bartley had said to her over the telephone. "My son is alive! Thank you, Lord. Oh thank you, Jesus!" she continued to cry aloud.

Cedric didn't answer his phone when she tried to reach him. She would have to let him know when he came to see her that evening. In the meantime, she had a new burst of energy. She put on her favorite Christmas music and started cleaning the home for the holiday. She moved the furniture and arranged it so the anticipated tree could have a place in the living room.

She had a new prayer to pray. "Lord, let him awake from his coma," she said. Rachel had a sense of faith that she had never known before. Since God was gracious to let her son be found, she had enough faith to believe that he would surely wake him up.

She heard the mail carrier outside and went to check the mail. She was moving faster than she had moved in days. She had so many advertisements for Christmas items. Other than a tree, she just didn't feel she needed anything else. Now she had her son. She was told that he was breathing and he was in a safe place.

Perusing the mail, she dropped ad after ad in the round trash can. Then she found a letter that unbelievably was from her son.

"What?" Rachel said as she plopped into the sofa chair. At first she was afraid to open it. She looked at the postmark and realized that it must have been the last letter sent before his latest mission. There's always a delay in receiving army mail during times of war or conflict. She knew he was somewhere in Iraq if he hadn't been reassigned. Rachel trembled as she held the letter to her chest. She wasn't sure if she had any more tears to free from her soul.

She gently turned the letter to its sealed side and opened it with her pointing finger. She smiled and let out a sigh as she looked at the handwriting that had always left her thinking she needed an analyst to interpret. She remembered telling him that he should have been a doctor.

> *Dear Mom,* the letter began.
> *Here I am again in the thick of things. I've been asked to go on a special mission. I can't tell you where I'm going exactly, but I want you to know that your boy has been selected to do something important. You know how I like a good challenge. Don't worry about the mission.*
> *I have prayed about it and I know that God will be with me.*
> *I wanted you to be the first to know that I have met a special girl. I really like her, but she's not where she should be in a spiritual sense. Her parents just didn't bring her up to know Jesus. I have dated her, and I have had the pleasure to plant some seeds about the love of God.*
> *Well, anyway, I just needed to tell somebody and I picked you. Her name, by the way, is Bonnie. I'm looking forward to introducing you to her one day.*
> *Until then, love your son,*
> *Charlie.*

Rachel closed her eyes tightly as she finished the letter. She felt a sense of confidence. If Charlie says it was God that led him to accept the assignment, then surely God would heal her son. She looked up at the sky and smiled. God was certainly in control. She felt the letter from Charlie was God's way of letting her know that he was in control. She just had to trust him through this ordeal. After all, she now knew it was God who took her through everything that happened thirty years ago. She began to reminisce about her life as a young woman. She was out of high school and living in her own little place. She had met a nice man and began dating him. Then they moved in together. Marriage wasn't a big deal because none of her friends were married. Her parents had been hippies and never married. The hippy era had an enormous effect on her town. She was just happy to have a good man around. The relationship produced two fine boys that were eighteen months apart. Her boyfriend did odd jobs to support the family. She loved the fact that no work was beneath him. He did whatever he could to keep food on the table.

SHE THOUGHT SHE WAS THE LUCKIEST GIRL AROUND. Then one day, he didn't come home. The police drove up to her apartment looking for Danny Smith. She told them she didn't know anyone with that name. They threatened to take her downtown and interrogate her, but she stuck to her story. They then showed the pictures they had of her with someone they called Danny Smith. She told them that was Greg. They said, "No ma'am. This person is Danny Smith."

Of course she was hurt that she lived with someone who had not trusted her to know his real name after three years. It turned out that Danny was living under an assumed name after breaking out of jail. He broke from a jail in California and settled in the Midwest. He made a mistake and used his social security number on his last job and the cops were hot on his trail.

She never had contact with him again. Three months later she read in the paper that he was killed in a shootout with police. She was devastated because she had lived for three years with a lie. When the children asked about their father growing up, she told them the truth. He was dead. She never told them how.

That seemed like a lifetime ago. She had sealed that part of her heart away. But recently she had given God her entire heart. It just needed a spiritual pacemaker. Finally the wound caused by deception could start to heal. She discovered that things that are hidden aren't necessarily healed. A nagging itch from an old scar could mean it didn't heal properly.

Rachel's mind came back to the present. She needed to concentrate her attention on Charlie and praying for his complete recovery.

Chapter Thirty-one

BONNIE BUTLER WAS ON A PLANE to Frankfurt, Germany. She thought it was incredible to be asked to accompany Charlie to the Frankfurt Medical Hospital. It wasn't that she had a lot of experience as God's servant, but she positively attributed this act to the hand of God. When the General asked her to take the assignment, he gave her 30 seconds to give him a reason that she couldn't do it. Two seconds after the shock had gone through her system, she said she'd be honored to accompany him. She would have been happy to pay them to take the assignment or to do it for free, but she was on the army's time clock for someone she felt deeply about.

They were transported in a Boeing C-47 cargo plane which was not configured for comfort. There were no luxury class seats. It could carry wounded men, or supplies, or even an army jeep. There were several other passengers needing medical attention, but Charlie was the only one severely wounded.

She just had to sit there and watch the medical assistant check his vitals every so often. The assistant checked the heartbeat and blood pressure while Bonnie prayed. The physicians were all optimistic. But since bombs send shrapnel everywhere, Charlie needed a complete body scan for detection.

There were three other soldiers being transported. One had his arm in a sling and the other was a young woman who recently discovered she was pregnant with twins. She was told to go on bed rest. Bonnie remembered the day the single mother-to-be came to see the Chaplain. Bonnie had seen a lot of unusual army circumstances. Her job was considered high level security because of the level of confidentiality that her office was sworn to uphold.

It was a long five-hour flight from Iraq to Frankfurt. Bonnie was sleepy but afraid to do anything but doze a little here and there. She had heard Charlie discuss his family when they first met, and she wondered how they were dealing with the situation.

She wondered if they knew that Charlie was a hero. According to the men he led, he took upon himself the most dangerous part of his job. He could have assigned it to someone else, but this mission had his name on it.

SHE KNEW THERE WAS SOMETHING SPECIAL about him from the first time they met. He wasn't afraid of anything. That in itself was scary to her. She didn't understand it at first, but she perceived that it was the peace of his God, whom she now belonged to, that kept him from being fearful.

The other army buddies looked up to him. He was a born leader. Soldiers automatically wanted to be like him.

"Prepare for landing," the pilot said on the speaker. Bonnie looked out the window and saw clouds that were hastily moving out of the way as if to introduce the city of Frankfurt. Bonnie was surprised to see the awesome skyscrapers amid the ancient looking castles in this international financial city. She was not sure what to expect, but this Germany was not the one she read about in history. It had somehow caught up with the rest of the world.

"Help me secure the patient," the attendant said to the man assisting him with Charlie's care. They took what resembled seatbelts of some sort and strapped him tightly to the bed. Pillows were put on both sides of his head.

Ten minutes later they were approaching the landing strip for a smooth touchdown. Bonnie saw a medical ambulance waiting near the tarmac. There were several cars parked alongside the ambulance with soldiers in full uniform awaiting to carry out their army orders. Two soldiers came aboard the flight to help with the lifting of the stretcher. The intravenous tubing was hand carried directly behind Charlie.

BONNIE FELT VERY SPECIAL. The hospital greeting included pomp and circumstance. She was saluted and asked to ride in the awaiting car which was to follow the ambulance. The first lieutenant and medical assistant were the first to deplane. He needed to transfer paperwork right away to the attending physicians.

Anxious to debark, he gathered his grip and stepped off the plane into a large wind gust that blew off his hat. He was about to salute the army officer meeting him. His nervousness must be responsible, thought Bonnie because he dropped his attaché case which was not secure. Papers immediately were flying around the young lieutenant's feet. Soldiers broke rank and left their positions to help gather the information. He was clearly embarrassed as he shoved it back down into the black briefcase.

The sirens were blasting, and that gave her an eerie feeling. Her emotions were all over the place. The reality set in that Charlie's life was on the line. She tried to get back in her comfort zone of believing that God was still in control of the situation and that Charlie would find his way back to the present conscious world.

Chapter Thirty-two

CEDRIC WAS SO HAPPY that he could hardly contain himself. He had just left his mother's house and heard the great news. His brother had been found. His mother's phone was ringing constantly with media calls, the mayor's office and even Charlie's friends. The story was now open to the public. Cedric advised his mother to check the caller identification slot and only answer official calls from the military.

He wanted to hop on an airplane and go straight to Germany, but the army asked them for 48 hours before making plans to come. They wanted to try some medication that had proven results for helping to awaken comatose patients. However, the medication worked best with no disturbances or distractions. Obviously, the army considered loved ones as possible interference with the project. Cedric and Rachel could have protested, but they wanted the best for their son and brother.

Cedric sometimes worked half days on Saturday. He found it necessary when the end of the month was approaching to make sure that all accounts were solvent for the bank. Today he had called off and would not be working on accounts. He would be trying to piece together a mystery.

He met Melissa and Buster at the Main Library and headed to the archives department.

"I heard the announcement about Charlie on the radio," Melissa said. "I hope he's better soon."

"Thanks," Cedric said.

Buster slapped him on the shoulder and said, "We're pulling for him."

Cedric acknowledged their well wishes by nodding his head. He was happy and anxious and emotional at the same time. He turned his attention to the investigation at hand.

He wasn't sure where to begin, but logic said to start with the year of the accident. They gathered around the computer. Melissa had a writing tablet and pen. They were serious young investigators with one mission.

"I've got a few theories on how to locate his children," Cedric said. "First we have to type in his name and the month of the accident."

"Do you know his real name?" Melissa asked.

"He was known all over the city as 'Stan the Ice Cream Man,'" Buster said.

"One of the ways my teacher taught me to search for information is with Ask.com," Melissa said. "She said there are more sophisticated ways to search, but unfortunately this library system is lagging behind," she continued.

Melissa typed in 'Stan the Ice Cream Man.' The results brought up a myriad of answers. Ice cream making machines, Mr. Stanley makes Creamy Cones, and a book on a little boy who grew up to sell ice cream machines.

"None of these are useful," Buster said. "How about ice cream vendor killed in accident?" he suggested.

Melissa typed in the information the way he proposed it. The computer slowly pulled up two things. 'Choose Saint Peter's Cemetery' and 'Ice Cream preacher succumbs to Fiery Death' both appeared.

The three of them stared at the last headline and felt eerie chills run down their spines. For a moment, none of them could speak. They were transported back in time to a horrible event in their childhood. Melissa could almost smell the black smoke that engulfed the truck. Buster could remember the last conversation with Mr. Stan, and Cedric could hear the sound of the fire engine roaring to get to the scene.

They clicked on the link of the headline and got a complete story. James Stanford Crosby, preacher and former Vietnam war hero, killed in car accident. Funeral–July 18, Mercy Christian Church.

129

Burial St. Peter's Cemetery. Survived by wife, June, and three children: Briana, Jackie and Joey M. Crosby.

"Well, that's more than we ever knew," Buster said. "My stomach's a little queasy."

"We've come this far," Cedric said. "I think we should dig a little further," he said matter-of-factly. Maybe we can get some information from the reporter that wrote this story. Even if it was twenty years ago."

"I think we should ask a librarian to help us," Melissa suggested. The two men nodded in agreement as Melissa got up from the computer to seek assistance.

THERE WERE TWO LADIES WORKING behind the desk. The younger woman was assisting two small children in checking out books. Melissa approached the older lady and interrupted her as she was writing notes into a binder.

"Excuse me," Melissa said. "Can you help us find some information?"

"I can try," the woman said in a voice that was a trained whisper. It seemed to suggest to Melissa that her voice should be lowered as well. Melissa led her to the computer where Cedric and Buster were located.

"We're trying to locate the descendants of a man who passed away about 20 years ago," Melissa said. "He sold ice cream from a truck in this city and was killed tragically in an accident," she explained.

The woman looked into the eyes of each of them with a strange sense of knowing. "Are you talking about Stanford Crosby?" she asked.

Melissa was stunned, and so were Cedric and Buster. "How did you know that?" Buster asked with amazement.

"He was my neighbor," she said with a smile. "He lived in the apartment up the street from me, and my children adored him. It was such a sad story," she said shaking her head. "His wife passed away a short time before he did," she said. "It was said to be some kind of lung disease or cancer."

Buster was in simple amazement. "Do you have any idea of what happened to the kids?" he blurted out.

"No, I don't," she said. "Sorry, I can't be of further help." She started walking away and quickly returned. "I just remembered," she said. "He was a member of Mercy Christian Church. You may want to go and see the pastor. That's where they had his funeral," she said.

"Thanks," Melissa said. "You've been a tremendous help."

Chapter Thirty-three

CHARLIE WAS TAKEN into an emergency holding room. There was a small glass window that Bonnie could take a peek through until she received her next orders. She was asked to have a seat in the waiting area. She selected a soft cushioned high back chair and closed her eyes for a moment. She was awfully sleepy because she forced herself to stay awake on the flight.

She was startled by a buzzing sound with someone speaking rapidly in German followed by the translation in English. Tired and edgy, she listened and watched attentively while men and women in white coats scrambled about to find wheelchairs and stretchers and head for the large opening in the emergency room.

A military airplane was landing with men needing immediate attention. It looked like all hands on deck. At least six stretchers were out and waiting with nearly that amount of wheelchairs. While they were all out, an attendant went into Charlie's room to give him blood. At first, he appeared to be looking for the attending nurse. Then he looked over the chart on the door, read the orders in his hand and hooked up the transfusion machine.

For the next two hours, the hospital was alive with every available medical person put in a life-saving mode. If Bonnie hadn't seen it herself, she would have thought it was a drill. As interesting as it was, she couldn't stand it any further and fell asleep.

IT WAS NOT A PEACEFUL REST. She dreamed a myriad of things, including hearing someone saying Charlie, cold blue. When Bonnie turned to change positions, she made an amazing discovery. The voices were not a part of the dream. There were doctors and nurses gathered in and out of the room where Charlie was resting.

132

He had gone into cardiac arrest.

Bonnie nearly fell jumping to her feet. She couldn't believe her eyes.

"Clear!" one of the doctors demanded as he applied the paddles to Charlie's chest. He repeated the function twice and only stopped when one of the female nurses said there was a heartbeat.

Tears streamed down Bonnie's face as she turned away from the scene and looked at the wall. She wasn't sure she could take much more. She left the waiting room to search out a restroom. Across from the restroom her eyes spotted a chapel. She recognized it by the cross on the front of the door. She headed for the chapel. From the outside it looked dark. She opened the door to find it empty. She wasn't sure what to do or say. She went between the benches and got down on her knees. Hoping that words would come, she closed her eyes and waited.

She wasn't sure what she was going to say, but finally the words came to mind. "Dear Lord," she began. "I don't really know what to say except please be merciful to Charlie. He's a good man and a great soldier," she explained. "Without him, I wouldn't have been introduced to you. He has given me a greater purpose to aspire. I know that you are powerful enough to spare his life." Then she repeated what she had heard the Chaplain say on numerous occasions. "I ask this in the name of your dear son, Jesus. Amen."

A CALMNESS CAME OVER HER as she used her right hand to wipe away the tears. She didn't know what would happen, but she knew God had heard her prayer. She got up and returned to the room after taking a short stop in the restroom. She was anxious to find out exactly what happened. She wished she could control situations, but she was only there to accompany him. She was doing her job. She decided to make some notes because she knew the military would want a full report.

The doctor eventually left Charlie and came to speak with Bonnie. "I'm Dr. Dubois and I'll be keeping an eye on the soldier for the rest of the night," he said.

"How is he now?" Bonnie asked in a hopeful tone.

"His condition is serious but stable," he said. "We'll keep a watchful eye during the next 24 hours."

"Will he have to get another transfusion?" she asked.

"What do you mean, another transfusion?" Dr. Dubois asked sternly.

"An attendant gave him a transfusion while the other doctors were admitting the soldiers from the last airplane," she explained.

With those words Dr. Dubois' eyes widened and he turned abruptly, as if he had just been given new orders. He rushed down the hall to the main nursing station. His voice could be heard over the intercom requesting certain personnel to meet with him.

Chapter Thirty-four

MELISSA GRABBED HER HEAD and seemed to massage the side temple.

"Are you ok?" Buster asked.

"I, I seem to have a migraine," Melissa answered closing her eyes momentarily.

"Can I get you some aspirin or pain medication?" he asked sincerely.

"No thanks!" both Melissa and Cedric answered simultaneously.

"I think I should just get something to eat and rest," Melissa explained. Buster looked from Melissa to Cedric seeking answers.

"Look, Buster," Cedric said. Why don't you take Melissa home so she can eat and rest?" he asked rhetorically.

"I'll pay a visit to the church to see if there's any more information on Mr. Stan," he said. "Plus I'm sure you want to spend more time with Melissa while you are here in town. I've got to find out if there is any more news on Charlie and see how Mama is doing too."

CEDRIC HAD PASSED MERCY CHRISTIAN CHURCH a number of times. He thought he would check it out since he was already out and about. Cedric had so much on his mind that he needed the drive to clear his head. In about 20 minutes he pulled up on the parking lot of the church. It wasn't very impressive at first glance. It probably held 250 people or less, but it did look inviting. The large stained glass window that centered the four pillows had a picture of Jesus with his arms inviting followers to himself. He was surrounded by sheep that appeared to have his full attention.

The faded yellow striping on the parking lot made it difficult to stay within the lines of his parking space. He was surprised by all the cars on the lot for a Saturday. Judging by the uneven spacing between cars, others were also having a difficult time staying within the faded lines.

Cedric got out of the car and noticed people began leaving the church. There were a number of children with their parents. He must have just missed a children's program, he thought to himself. He entered the edifice and heard a little boy, who appeared to be around seven or eight years old, singing "Silent Night." He realized he had come just in time for the completion of a Christmas program rehearsal.

"Excuse me," he said to the little boy's parent, "where can I find the pastor?"

"I saw him peeking in on the rehearsal a few moments ago," the young lady stated. "Try his office. It's down this hallway on the right," she said pointing in the direction on the left side of the main sanctuary.

Cedric found the office and knocked on the door.

"Come in," a deep but gentle voice replied.

"Hello Reverend," Cedric said extending his arm for a handshake. "My name is Cedric Grimes and I have some questions that I hope you can answer for me," he said.

"If it's the name of the twelve apostles, I can help you, but if it's why God allows suffering in the world, I'll refer you to the church down the street," he said laughing. "I'm Pastor Brownlee."

His response completely took Cedric off guard and made him laugh too. "No sir," Cedric replied. "It's not quite that deep. I'm looking for some information on the children of a man who I knew as a child. He sold ice cream from a truck about 20 years ago and was killed suddenly."

"James Stanford Crosby," Rev. Brownlee said. "Why are you interested in him?" he asked.

"It's kind of a long story, Reverend," Cedric explained. "Do you have a few minutes?"

"Pull up a chair, son," Reverend Brownlee said. "You're not a news reporter, are you?" he questioned.

"No, sir. I was one of the last people to see Mr. Stan before he died," he said in a voice just above a whisper.

Reverend Brownlee began to see the gravity of the meeting. "You must have been quite young, son," he said.

"I was about seven years old," Cedric said. "It was quite a traumatic experience. My brother and I, along with two other kids who were my neighbors, were in line to get ice cream and to spin for a prize. Mr. Stan was out of prizes, except he did give my neighbor a little ring. But he gave the three of us who were left some pamphlets called 'tickets to heaven.' One of the things he said when he gave them to us was that he planned to give them to his children. It's been 20 years, and my neighbors and I decided we wanted to make good on his last wish. I know it's strange, but we still have the pamphlets. It would help bring closure to a painful memory. Hopefully, it would be a blessing to the receivers," Cedric said sounding like an attorney giving closing remarks.

"Wow," Reverend Brownlee said rubbing his balding head. "That's quite a story."

The reverend opened his desk drawer and pulled out a rolodex. He began looking through the cards in the mid-section. "Honestly, son, I wasn't the pastor 20 years ago, but I have heard mentions of Mr. Crosby from time to time. I've been here about 15 years, and one thing I know for sure," he said looking up, "if anybody knows anything about the history of the members, it's Sister Fannie Mason. Some people call her a busybody, but I call her a historian. She doesn't forget anything. She's kind of eccentric."

Reverend Brownlee picked up his telephone to call the number on the card.

"Sister Mason?" he asked. "Oh, you knew it was me. That caller ID takes all the surprise from making calls," he said laughing. "I have a young man in my office that needs some information that I think you might be able to help him with. He's needing some information on the family of James Stanford Crosby. Yes, the ice cream man."

You don't mind? Uh huh. Hold on a minute," he said covering the talking piece of the phone. "She wants to know if you can come over now because she's got a birthday party tonight," Reverend Brownlee said.

"Absolutely," Cedric answered, hoping it wasn't too far away. He knew he needed to check on things with his mom concerning Charlie.

"Alright, he'll be there shortly," Reverend Brownlee said. "God bless you. Goodbye."

"She lives about two miles away," he said as if he had been reading Cedric's mind.

The reverend wrote the address on a small tablet, ripped it off and handed it to Cedric. "Son, I think what you're doing is admirable. Godspeed."

"Thank you, sir," Cedric replied, shook his hand and left the office.

Chapter Thirty-five

BONNIE BUTLER WAS GIVEN A PERSONAL ESCORT to the hospitality building where she would be staying during her assignment with Charlie. It was only two city blocks away from the hospital, so she considered walking the distance if the weather was cooperative.

Charlie's condition was stable when she left, although she was reluctant to leave him alone. She knew that she needed to get some sleep, so she didn't resist much when told it was time to leave.

She missed Chaplain Bartley. He was a great person to talk to, and she now considered him a spiritual leader for her new journey. Bonnie found the room she was given quite comfortable. After her shower, she climbed in bed and thought she would read her Bible for a few minutes before shutting down for the night. She opened the book to Psalm 118. When she got to the 17th verse, she meditated on it and thought of Charlie.

Bonnie's face rubbed against the leaves of her Bible. Someone was knocking on her door. She tried to compose herself as she got up to answer the door.

"Who is it?" Bonnie asked.

"It's your car service, ma'am. I'm a little early, but I was told to come and get you quickly."

Bonnie was confused but went straight to the window to pull open the heavy curtain and blind. She was shocked to see the daylight. She then went to get her watch from the nightstand and saw that it was 0700 hours. She had no idea she had been asleep all night. She wondered what was wrong because she was not supposed to be picked up until 0900 hours.

"I'll be out in 20 minutes," she said to the driver as she looked out the peephole.

"Thank you, ma'am. I'll have coffee waiting for you," the driver said.

Bonnie removed a fresh uniform from her garment bag and dressed as quickly as possible. She had done everything including her light makeup in eighteen minutes.

"Do you know what's going on?" she asked the driver as she slid into the vehicle.

"I'm sorry," her driver said. "I wasn't given any details. Only told to pick you up right away."

Bonnie's heart sunk. She had been so hopeful for a recovery that she hadn't thought of facing unfavorable news. She rushed inside to the elevator and noticed no one was on it. It was eerily quiet, but it was still very early. Bonnie bowed her head and said a prayer. All she could think to say was, "Lord have mercy!"

She approached the nursing station but kept going until she reached Charlie's room. There were three people surrounding his bed. Two were in white coats and one was in a uniform. She slowed as she approached to brace herself. Peeking between the two doctors, she saw Charlie's eyes opened and a smile on his face. She thought she would faint from the suspense, but she remembered that she was a soldier and composed herself.

"Hello, soldier," she said.

"Hello, major," he replied in a raspy voice. "Where have you been?" he asked.

Bonnie smiled and saw that the uniformed soldier was taking note. "Just following you around, soldier," she said staring at the doctor for answers. The doctor beckoned for her to step into the hallway.

"We were able to give him another transfusion late last night," he said. "There was a mix up with the paperwork and he had received the wrong type of blood. Several hours after the transfusion, there were signs of cognizance with movement in his fingers and mouth twitching. In another two hours he was awake. We want to transfer him back to the states for continual observation, but we think he's out of the woods. We're pretty busy here. If you don't have any objection, I'd like to recommend you continue your escort to his home state. The hospital has already been made aware of his coming in two days."

Bonnie's eyes glistened to think she would be back in the states during the Christmas season. Even if it was for official business, this was one of the greatest presents she could get for the holiday.

"I'll make ready, sir," she said saluting the doctor. "We'll give you a few minutes alone to question him about the combat," the doctor said. "But remember, no badgering, he is still fragile and needs lots of rest."

"Not a problem, sir," Bonnie replied. "I also request permission to contact his family," she said.

"Permission granted," the doctor replied. He then motioned for the others to leave the room as Bonnie pulled a tablet from her purse with a pen and sat in the chair by his bed.

"Are you able to talk about your last memory?" she asked Charlie.

"I know I remember putting Hutson in charge," he said. "There was something I needed to do, but it's kind of cloudy right now," he continued.

"Can I do anything for you?" Bonnie asked.

"Please let my mother know that I'm ok," he said. "She might be worried about me."

"Consider it done, soldier," she said. "Anything else?"

"Yeah, there's this soldier I've been seeing. Her name's Bonnie Beautiful. If you see her, tell her she's got a special ticket of mine. I want her to keep it safe," he said.

"I'll tell her," Bonnie said. "I better let you get some rest. Your memory seems to be just fine."

Charlie smiled and fell into a light sleep.

Chapter Thirty-six

BUSTER WATCHED as Melissa slowly devoured a bowl of soup. She didn't want him to buy her any fast food. She just wanted to come home and eat and maybe lie down.

"Are you sure you're ok?" Buster asked. "I carry pain medicine in my wallet," he said.

"I can do this without the medicine," she insisted.

"But it's quicker if…" he began.

"No, Buster," Melissa said louder than she intended. "I can't take any drugs," she confessed. "I used to be addicted to pain medicine. There. I said it. I didn't want you to know. I hid it from everyone for at least 10 years," she said.

"How did I not know this? How did you get addicted to pain medicine?" Buster asked.

"It started with the nightmares from Mr. Stan's accident," she began. "I couldn't rest at night. I was always afraid. We never really talked about his accident. Mama always changed the subject to protect us, but we never got closure and it was hard for a child my age to see something so horrible and never discuss it. It didn't go away. I used to take some of Mama's pain pills when she first got sick," she said.

"What? I had no idea," Buster said.

"I was afraid to tell anyone. But they made me feel better. No one knew that on top of all that, Marvin sometimes touched me inappropriately," she said a little gentler.

"He did what?" Buster said getting angry. "Why didn't you tell Mama? Why didn't you tell me?" he said kneeling next to her at the table. "I would have found a way to protect you," he said with a tear streaming down his face. "I promise you I would have never let him get near you."

"You were always my Superman Brother," Melissa said. "I was so wounded, I couldn't cry. Sometimes wounded people just bleed," she said grabbing his hand. "Our bleeding is internal and only God can heal our hurt."

Buster stood up and shook his head. "I guess things weren't much better at Aunt Macey's home for us either. I don't know why our uncle drank himself to death. Did you know Aunt Macey is now in a nursing home?" Buster asked.

"No," Melissa said in a surprised voice. "When I left a few years ago, I never looked back. I kept thinking that there's got to be a better ending to my life's story. These past few weeks, though, Cedric has proved that my life isn't over or headed downward. I think I can smile again from the inside. I just have to stay away from medicine and face life head on. Will you help me Buster?" she asked.

"You got it, sis," he said. "From now on, we're going to keep in touch and I will do everything I can to make your life better," he said. "I owe you that much. After the holidays, I want to go visit Aunt Macey. I want to tell her about Jesus and let her know that we are not harboring any ill feelings. I think she would appreciate that," he said.

"I'd like to go with you," Melissa said. "I believe that will be a part of my journey to have a better future."

"Speaking of futures," Buster said with a smile, "you have got to meet Grace. She is so wonderful and caring and beautiful. I know I've mentioned her on the phone, but I want you to meet in person. Hey, by the way, she's got the ticket to heaven. I will try to persuade her to come here for a couple of days to meet you. At one time we discussed coming to visit you. I'm sure she's got plenty of airline miles to get a reduced rate, and I can drive her back. She would be great company on the road."

"I really would like to meet her," Melissa said. "I just wish Mom could have lived to see us get married and have children. I'll be so happy to have a sister. Because of all we endured as children, I feel like life has got to have more to offer."

"It does, and I've got a feeling things are going to turn around real soon for you," Buster said.

"What do you mean?" Melissa asked.

"I think Cedric is kind of sweet on you," he said.

"Oh, well, he's my other hero," she said smiling. "I know you know about the rehab center he helped me to get in, but I don't think you knew he bailed me out of jail."

"What?" Buster said. "Why were you in jail?"

"It's a long story, but sit down and I'll tell you all about it," she said.

Chapter Thirty-seven

IT WAS AN OFFICIAL CALL and the news was good. "I don't know why I'm so nervous," Bonnie said to herself. But deep down Bonnie knew that her personal feelings for Charlie had become so intermingled with her duties that she wasn't quite sure where one ended and one began. She was grateful that God had answered her prayer. In the back of her mind, she was almost blaming her parents for not seeking to find out that God truly existed while she was a child. They had deprived her of a spiritual relationship that was more than words could describe. But, instead, she felt sorry for them and was just grateful that she now knew the truth. She promised God that she would read his word every day to make up for lost time.

"Here goes nothing," she said aloud as she read the official contact information from Charlie's military paperwork. She made the call while simultaneously practicing deep breathing exercises in order to calm her nerves. The phone rang only twice before it was picked up with a sound of anxiousness.

"Hello?" Rachel answered as if it were a question. "Hello, this is Major Butler. May I speak with Rachel Grimes?"

"This is she," Rachel answered as her hand began to sweat holding the telephone receiver.

"Mrs. Grimes, I have to give you an official update on your son, Charlie Grimes," Bonnie began. "I have good news for you. Charlie has awakened from his coma and is alert and talking," she reported. "I have even better news," she continued. "In a few days he will be transferred to the army hospital near your city. I have been assigned to accompany him," she said.

"Oh, oh thank God," Rachel responded trembling. "Thank God. God is a prayer-answering God," she said with great emotion.

"Yes, he is," Bonnie responded.

"When can I talk to him?" Rachel asked. "Is there any memory loss?" she questioned.

"Well, I'm not a physician," Bonnie answered in a tone meant to calm Rachel. "There are good signs. But he will be under a doctor's care for a while longer, even when he returns."

"Did you say you were accompanying him?" Rachel asked.

"Yes ma'am, I did," she answered.

"What did you say your name was?" Rachel asked.

"Major Butler, Bonnie Butler," she clarified.

Rachel's eyes widened as she remembered the name in the letter. "Well Bonnie, when you're back in the states, please come visit me if it's alright with your superiors. I'm going to plan a welcome home party for Charlie. If it's not against the rules, please come by and see me. I just want to thank you for your service," Rachel said.

"That's not necessary," Bonnie interjected. "It's part of my duty."

"Oh, please come by anyway, if you don't have to leave right away. I'd love to meet you," Rachel pleaded.

"I'll do my best," Bonnie promised. "Until then, take care Mrs. Grimes," Bonnie said before hanging up the phone.

Chapter Thirty-eight

CEDRIC FOLLOWED THE DIRECTIONS exactly as they were written and pulled up in front of 5700 Gladiola Avenue. The house was a one-story bungalow with neatly trimmed bushes that were starting to die out for the winter. Dried-up Morning Glories and a dark green ivy plant ran up the pathway and took a sharp turn to the right where they found a path on the house guttering.

The neighbors' houses were more modern with additions on at least three of them. Cedric had seen that before. Someone would come to the bank to apply for a loan because they wanted to keep up with the improvements initiated by their neighbors. This time Cedric took paper and pen with him. He always kept a tablet in his glove compartment. The pens were in several locations of his car, and they all were monogrammed with the bank's logo. He had barely knocked on the six-panel oak door when it opened and a woman no more than four feet ten appeared. She was dressed in a fancy suit with a mink-like fur collar and a golden broach. The warmth of the room suggested she had thin blood even for December. Other than her mingled gray wig that was slightly off-center, she looked impeccable.

"I'm Cedric Grimes; Reverend Brownlee sent me to speak with you," Cedric said to break the silence. Mrs. Mason smiled a broad smile and revealed two golden teeth on the right side of her mouth that were shining replacements for those that were no longer there.

"Come on in," Mrs. Mason directed. "My granddaughter will be picking me up in about an hour, so you caught me just in time," she said.

"Yes, ma'am," Cedric replied. "I understand you have a party to get to."

"I sure do," she said motioning for him to take a seat on her olive-green couch. It was covered in a heavy-duty plastic to ensure its longevity.

"My beautician is turning 80, and Clara would have a fit if I didn't attend her party," Mrs. Mason said. "You know she's been doing my hair for 43 years."

"Wow!" Cedric said, wondering how much hair she really had since she was wearing the gray wig.

"Don't let this hairpiece fool you," Mrs. Mason said. "Clara can still do some hair. I just didn't feel like fooling with it today," she explained."

CEDRIC DECIDED TO GET STARTED with the reason he had come to see her. He was almost afraid that the elderly woman could read his mind.

"Mrs. Mason," he began, "I was about seven years old when Mr. Stan the Ice Cream Man would frequent the park in my old neighborhood. I was there with my brother and some neighborhood friends when he was killed. The reason I want to find Mr. Stan's children is that he gave me something that he originally wanted them to have," he explained.

"Like what?" Mrs. Mason asked with her curiosity getting the best of her.

"Tickets to heaven," Cedric said. "I believe they were pamphlets used for witnessing. Because of the circumstances of his death, we, my brother and our friend, just held on to them. Of course, that's been 20 years ago. He gave them to us because he was out of prizes. He told us he had been saving them for his children. It was just a few moments later that the terrible accident occurred."

"Lord have mercy," Mrs. Mason said shaking her head. "Would you like some hot chocolate and cookies?" Cedric wasn't sure how he should answer her question. He didn't have a grandmother, so he wasn't sure if it would be an insult to say no or if accepting her kind gesture would help him get more information from her. So, he chose the latter.

"If it's not too much trouble," he said. "That sounds good."

She smiled that very expensive golden smile and told him to have a seat at her kitchen table.

He moved into the kitchen and watched her meticulously level a scoop and a half of cocoa mix into a beautiful coffee mug while she heated water in a well-aged black kettle. The whistling kettle alerted her that the water was hot, and she retrieved the cookies from a bear-molded cookie jar. The tip of the left brown ear was chipped. Cedric imagined that the jar must have had great sentimental value, otherwise this lady that he hardly knew would not have it among her very neat glasses and kitchenware.

He thanked her and bit into the oatmeal raisin cookie.

"I'll be right back," she said. He took a sip of the beverage, and just for a moment he thought, "This must be what it's like to have a loving grandmother." Mrs. Mason returned with a scrapbook in her hand. She turned several pages and finally looked up. Here is a photograph of our last church picnic with Mr. Stan," she said. Cedric put the cocoa down and pushed away the cookies.

"The cookies are delicious," he said, remembering his manners.

"You got a wife?" Mrs. Mason asked flashing her smile.

"No, ma'am," he answered politely.

"Cause a man who gives compliments so freely will soon have a ring on his finger. Too bad my granddaughter's already married. I would have made her acquainted with you," she said with a cautious laugh.

"This is Mr. Stan, this is his wife and here are their three children," she said pointing to each figure in the picture.

IT WAS A GROUP SHOT of about 50 people in five long rows with the first row of people sitting on a picnic bench. "This was about two months before the accident," she said. "I remember it like it was

149

yesterday. It was our annual May picnic. Mr. Stan hadn't long been returned from the military service. He had been back maybe three years. He came back and joined the church. I knew that he had some type of disability that kept him from reenlisting. Sometimes he would drag his leg a little. So, he took up driving the ice cream truck in the summer. At first it was a temporary job until his permanent disability checks started to come in. Then he decided he liked talking to people, especially children. He always talked about going to heaven. Sometimes people said he was a little strange because he talked about angels a lot. I know all this because I offered to keep the kids while his wife looked for work," she said shaking her head. "The poor thing found out she had some type of cancer and died just six weeks later. It was such a tragedy. First the mother, then the father. Those poor kids."

"What happened to them?" Cedric asked, finishing up his cookie and seemingly mesmerized by her story. Cedric decided that Mrs. Mason must not have heard his question. She stared at the photo as if she was transported back in time.

"Now this tall gentleman," she said with sentiment, "is my late husband, Ralph. He's been gone the better part of ten years now," she explained.

"You must miss him a lot," Cedric said, feeling comfortable enough to comment.

"I suppose," Mrs. Mason said with a sigh.

Cedric took another bite of his cookie. "What do you miss most?" he continued.

Mrs. Mason had a twinkle in her eye when she responded. "When he passed, I missed his kisses, his complimenting me when I cooked, his accompanying me to engagements, his calling me from work just to check on me," she said.

"Wow, he did all those things?" Cedric asked rhetorically.

"He did none of those things," she snapped. "That's why I said I missed them!" Mrs. Mason gave out a grunt. "Let's not get started on Ralph the Rascal," she said.

Cedric quickly returned his attention to the matter before them. "Do you know what happened to Mr. Stan's children?" he asked for the second time.

"Sadly, they had no next of kin and went into a foster care home," Mrs. Mason answered. "By the grace of God, the girls were adopted by a local family. The family only had one extra bedroom, though, so they only took the girls. The little boy was a twin to one of the girls, but unfortunately he kept getting passed over and moved around from one foster home to another. I don't know where he is. The girls are all grown up and every now and then visit the church. I know because they were adopted by Mr. and Mrs. Hamilton. I don't know where they live in town, but Mr. Hamilton owns a dry cleaners business on West Main."

Cedric was so thrilled he wanted to kiss Mrs. Mason. Instead, he opted to give her a great big hug. "Thank you so much, Mrs. Mason. You have been a wealth of knowledge. God bless you," he said. "With your help, this may be a bright Christmas after all." He left feeling as if God had given him this mission to help take his mind off his brother Charlie's condition.

Chapter Thirty-nine

BRIANA WATCHED THROUGH the shop's window as Mrs. Patterson lifted the basket of clothes from the car, instructed her son to wait for her and proceeded to enter the dry cleaners. Her timing was perfect and an indication that it must be Thursday. It was the same request each week. She would need five uniforms washed and pressed to be picked up on Saturday. Since Mrs. Patterson began this weekly routine, she was so used to it that she could have completed the task with her eyes closed. Perhaps she did close them for a moment or just blinked. Whatever the excuse was, she didn't see the man pull beside her, jump out of the car and head for the door. They collided, and her hospital uniform ended up hanging from his arm as if he were the maître d`. He apologized, then she apologized and they both kept coming toward the door. She was in a hurry. He was in a hurry, and both of them wanted to go through the single door first. She was a customer and he was a delivery driver. He had a set schedule and she thought he should be a gentleman. There appeared to be an impasse. But another customer was leaving through the exit only door. So, the delivery driver entered that door as a compromise.

"Delivery for Briana Hamilton," the driver said.

"Just one moment, Mrs. Patterson," Briana said nicely as she walked toward the delivery driver.

"Sign here," he said handing a pen to her. The name and address read: Briana Hamilton, c/o Hamilton Cleaners. The return address said: Adoption, Research and More. Briana's heart skipped a beat as she put the envelope aside to wait on Mrs. Patterson. She was in such a hurry to get back to the envelope that she almost forgot to ask if she had coupons. She then completed the order, retrieved the envelope and headed to the back of the cleaners.

"Cover the desk for a moment, Nicole," she yelled out. "I have to go into the office for a few moments."

Chapter Forty

"OH MY GOD!" Grace said responding to the story Buster told of finding out who Stan the Ice Cream Man really was. "You guys make great detectives," she continued. "I wish I could have been there."

"Well, that's the other reason I'm calling," Buster said. "I want you to come down and spend a few days with me. You'll get to officially meet Melissa, and I want you to meet my friend Cedric. He and his mom are having a hard time right now because of Cedric's brother, Charlie. First, he was missing in Iraq, he was found and then he went into a coma. They could really use some cheering up. I've also found out some hurtful things that were going on with my sister. I don't want to say a lot about it, but she suffered some abuse," Buster relayed. "It makes me feel like I failed her as a brother," he confessed.

"Buster, you're not God," Grace said. "So don't go on a guilt trip about things you had no control over. Everybody I know that lived to adulthood has experienced some tragedy in one way or another. And guess what? It's a part of life. All of us have our 'why me' moments in this life. We all want the happily ever after. But even Cinderella suffered first, and I guarantee you if we saw the second half of her life, there would be another cross for her to bear."

"Wow!" Buster responded. "You make a pretty good counselor. I felt your sincerity all the way here," he said. "This is going to be a great holiday. Call me when you know when you're coming. I've got to go now. I'm meeting Cedric this evening. I love you."

"I love you too," Grace said.

"Hey! Don't forget to bring your ticket to heaven," he said and hung up the phone.

CEDRIC LEFT SEVERAL MESSAGES when he called Hamilton Dry Cleaners, but the answering machine kept cutting him off. It had constantly malfunctioned to the point that Cedric decided to wait a few hours, hoping that someone would realize no calls were getting through. He tried calling one more time when a young, sweet voice picked up and answered.

"Hamilton Cleaners," Nicole answered.

"Hello, my name is Cedric Grimes. I'm trying to locate the children or the daughters of the owner," he said.

"Is this for a debt collection?" Nicole asked suspiciously.

"Oh no, nothing like that," he said. "I have something that belongs to the daughters, and I want to return it," he explained.

"Hold on a moment," Nicole said. Cedric was hoping not to get a dial tone in his ear. He was as forthcoming as he could be.

"Hello, this is Briana," a pleasant voice greeted him.

"Hello, Briana," Cedric said. "Do you have a few moments to spare?" he asked.

"What's this about?" she asked.

"It's sort of a long story, but ..."

"Hey, listen," Briana said, "I don't have time to play games. Tell me what you want or I'm hanging up," she demanded.

"Oh no," Cedric exclaimed. "Ok, a long time ago I knew your father," he began.

"Everybody knows my father," Briana answered. "He's been in the dry cleaning business for years."

"I meant your real father," Cedric continued. "I knew Mr. Stan. He gave me and my brother and a friend a gift, but he said it was originally intended for his children. Minutes later he was killed in an accident," he said.

There was silence on the phone for about a moment. "I get off at 6 p.m. Can you meet me at the coffee shop at 4th and Pine at 6:30?" she asked.

"I'll be there," Cedric promised. "I'll be the one reading a newspaper among technology geeks. If that doesn't work," he added, "I'll have on my black tennis shoes."

Chapter Forty-one

BONNIE HAD MIXED EMOTIONS as the airplane left the runway. Charlie's last night at the hospital had been restless. His vital signs were holding steady, so the doctor diagnosed anxiety as the chief cause for his sleeplessness and jittery movements. He was tucked into his traveling bed like a little child and with the help of a mild sedative was fast asleep. Bonnie knew she would be landing at Scott Air Force Base in about 8 hours. Then, they would take an ambulance another two hours to the Veterans Hospital. If Charlie continued his health improvements, they would release him on Christmas eve.

Bonnie was just a little anxious herself. She had never been to Illinois and she certainly was not sure about meeting Charlie's mom. She imagined many things about her and wondered if it was a good idea to meet her. She hoped that his mother was unaware that she and Charlie had begun a relationship. Before her confession to be a Christian, she thought she was more sophisticated than Charlie and therefore in a great position to be the one to call the shots. But since her conversion, she felt unworthy to be linked with him. She considered him a war hero and a great Christian example. Bonnie reminisced about high school. She used to tease her classmates because they were Christians. Her parents had taught her that it was a sign of weakness to feel the need for a higher power. They told her that they had done just fine depending on their knowledge and wisdom. She could hardly wait to tell her father that she had encountered someone much greater than knowledge and earthly wisdom. She had experienced the love of God. Bonnie wrapped her arms around herself. Just thinking about Jesus gave her a special type of goose bumps. Only a God could love me like this, she thought to herself.

MEETING CHARLIE WAS SO SPECIAL. She didn't want to rush their relationship. But there were things she felt that he should know about her family. She didn't want to go deeper into a relationship with him unless he understood what he was getting into. She still felt renewed and clean since her conversion experience and didn't want him to feel deceived once he found out more about her atheist family. But for now, she just praised God for the miracle of Charlie's recovery. There would be plenty of time to tell her life's story.

Chapter Forty-two

TEARS STREAMED DOWN CEDRIC'S FACE while he embraced his mother. He felt he had become a cry-baby. He wanted to squeeze her even tighter than he was doing. He didn't want to hurt her, but the news that his brother was alert and coming home just overwhelmed him. Even though he had been purposely busy to keep his mind from concentrating on Charlie's condition, it was always right in the forefront of his mind. Whenever he was alone the past few nights, he entertained the idea that he might lose his brother.

"Now I can't waste any time," his mother said moving toward the kitchen table. "I've started a list of what we need for Charlie's homecoming party. I need a banner this wide," she said stretching out her arms. "I want to put it outside, above the door. I need a Christmas ham and all the fixin's and ..."

"Now, Mom, don't overdo it," Cedric warned. "You don't want to be too tired to enjoy the family or your guests," he explained.

"Oh, I know," Rachel said. "But I've got to get this spare bedroom in order, and do you think you could lend your card table?" she asked.

"I think I may have to lend you two card tables," Cedric answered. "See, Mom, earlier today I met with Bernard and Melissa—yes, both of Ms. Christina's children are in town. I wanted to invite them over but more importantly a couple of others. Remember when I told you what Mr. Stan said to us that awful day!"

"Are you talking about the part where he mentioned his kids?" she asked. "Absolutely."

"Well, Mom," I have located one of three of the kids. As a matter of fact, I have to meet her in a few hours. She and her sister both live in town, and I'm asking them to come over on Christmas to see all of us," he said proudly.

"Oh my," Rachel said smiling. "That would be wonderful! I'd better get more food!"

"Wow, I feel like God has really smiled on us to allow my brother to come home alive," he said. "Have you spoken to him, Mom?"

"No, I'm very anxious too, but now they are on their way back to the states."

"So, do we pick him up from the hospital or air force base? What's the deal?" Cedric inquired.

"Actually, the government assigned someone to accompany him."

"Does he have all his limbs, Mom?" Cedric asked. "You know sometimes the government won't tell you everything over the phone," he warned.

"I didn't actually ask that question, but the army lady I spoke with didn't appear to be hiding anything," she said looking serious. Her expression quickly changed to a more pleasant one. "I refuse to believe that God would bring him this far through answered prayer, then shock us. I think he is going to be just fine."

Chapter Forty-three

BRIANA DROVE THE WHITE CHEVY SEDAN slowly as she took the trip to meet Cedric at the popular coffee shop. It felt surreal that someone would contact her about her father. She was only six when he passed away.

She didn't remember a whole lot about him, but she had warm feelings whenever the memories flooded her mind. She knew he loved her and her brother and sister. As a child, she never understood his sudden departure. First her mother left her suddenly, then her daddy was gone too. Her life was very confused as a child. She remembered attending kindergarten with her mother holding her hand and telling her it would be alright. She remembered not going to school because her mother was suddenly gone and her daddy hugging her and the other children tightly as he wept. It was a vague memory. But it never left her completely. She remembered adjusting to just having her daddy and a babysitter. Then the babysitter and a policeman were having an intense discussion one evening. There were other strangers coming to her house. She recognized some of the people from church. She just had no idea of what was happening until the pastor of the church surrounded by two ladies tried to explain to her that her daddy was not coming home.

Anxiety was causing Briana's heart to pound as she began to relive the memories. A driver blew his horn from the car behind her. She was unaware that the light had turned green. She continued her slow journey to her appointment and the driver went around her.

What could this stranger she spoke with have for her that she was unaware of for so many years? For her sixteenth birthday, her adoptive parents had given her a locket and ring that had belonged to her birth mother. Her sister was given a bracelet that was their mother's. Her parents explained the best way they could the tragic circumstances leading to their adoption. While they always knew they were adopted, the new parents waited nearly ten years to discuss the details. They wanted to put some distance between the traumatic situation to give the children an opportunity to have a normal life.

WHILE BRIANA APPRECIATED THEIR CONCERN, she wondered for years why she had certain memories but was afraid to address it with her parents. She was grateful for their love and tried to always be an obedient child, because in her mind she felt like they might abandon her as well.

She treasured her mother's jewelry. The only thing she had belonging to her father was an American Flag that she was given at his death. She remembered a tall soldier handing it to her at the cemetery. It traveled with her to the foster home and accompanied her to the new adoptive parents' home. It stayed in a box folded ever so neatly. She was told as a little girl that the flag was something to be proud of because her daddy worked hard to defend it. She was not sure why, but this always made her smile.

Briana turned the final corner and was at the coffeehouse. Street parking was plentiful at this time of the evening, and feeding the meter was unnecessary. She had an uneasy feeling that she was about to come face to face with questions that had haunted her from a distance for the last twenty years.

Briana walked through the cafe door and stood to the side. Three men and one woman made eye contact with her. She ignored the woman and eliminated the old man with the beard. That left two young men whose tables were relatively close. Briana moved forward, and her eyes fell on the tennis shoes deliberately sticking out from under the table. She smiled back at the young man and approached his table.

"Hi, I'm Briana," she said warmly.

"I'm Cedric," a voice from behind her answered. Briana turned and saw Cedric heading toward her from the restroom area. He indeed had on black tennis shoes. The man she introduced herself to had on dark grey tennis shoes and was working on his laptop.

"Excuse me," Briana said as an apology for the mix-up.

"This way," Cedric said pointing to a corner table where there was an open newspaper.

"Oh my goodness," Briana said. "I forgot you mentioned a newspaper."

When they got to the corner table she extended her hand.

"I'm Briana," she said. "I thought I better introduce myself actually looking at you in the face."

"I'm happy to meet you," Cedric said shaking her hand. "Would you like some coffee or tea?" he said as they took their seats.

"No thanks," Briana said. "I prefer to get right to the point," she said nicely but in a matter of fact way. "I don't have a lot of memories of my father, but the ones I do have are vivid," she began. "He was a loving father. He worked a lot, but he always brought me and my siblings a treat when he came home. Sometimes it was ice cream and sometimes it was jelly beans."

"He sounds like a great man, Briana," Cedric said. "I'm glad you have memories of him. My father also died when I was young, but I can't recall much about him at all. My brother Charlie and I went to the park whenever our mom had time to take us. We usually teamed up with our neighbor and her son and daughter. We called ourselves the three musketeers. We loved to play on the park's old swing set. I don't know if they have it in the park anymore. That particular day, we heard the music for the ice cream truck and we went running to get money from our mothers. That part I remember just like it was yesterday. We wanted to spin for a prize or something like that. So, when we got to the truck to place our order, we were told that he was out of prizes. I remember being so disappointed. I mean your dad gave us cool stuff. I liked the tattoos and once I got a whistle," Cedric said laughing and reminiscing simultaneously.

"But this particular day our friend Melissa got a ring, and this is where it gets interesting. Mr. Stan told us that he was out of prizes, but he had something better. He handed the three of us, which was me, my brother Charlie and my friend Buster, some tickets. He seemed reluctant to give them to us at first. He said he was saving them for his own kids.

"What did they look like?" asked Briana. "Did you bring it?" she asked anxiously.

"I loaned mine to a friend, but she's going to bring it back so you can have it," he promised. "The front of the pamphlet said 'Ticket to Heaven.' There were instructions on how to use the ticket and he had just three left."

"That's amazing," Briana said. "There are exactly three of us."

"I know it's not silver or gold," Cedric said, "but he was thinking of his children during his last moments on earth. I thought you would want to know that."

"Actually, it's more valuable than money," Briana said. "It's more of a legacy that connects us as a family from this world to the next," she said wiping away a tear. "There's no doubt in my mind that he loved his family and I thank you for taking the time to share this information with me."

"I understand that your sister lives in town," Cedric said.

"She does, and I can hardly wait to tell her. This is such amazing information and so timely. I've been searching for my brother for months, and today of all days, I get an answer from the company that I hired to look for him. He's been located, and they are sending him my request to call me or visit me. I gave them all my information. I feel like I have an early Christmas present."

"Well, my friend is bringing the ticket to my mom's on Christmas Day. My mom would like to have you and your sister come to a Christmas dinner. It will be special because we expect my brother to arrive. He was injured in Iraq and is hopefully coming home that day. It would make the day very special for us. My friend Buster plans to bring his ticket as well. It's amazing that we both kept them for twenty years."

"I'd love to come," Briana said. "I feel like a large piece of my life's puzzle has been filled in," she said.

"I hope everything works out for your brother to see you. Here's mom's address," Cedric said writing it down.

"Well, it would be the first step in making our family whole again," Briana said. "I appreciate everything my adoptive parents did by taking us in, but the day we were separated as children, I felt like a little bit of me died that day. I know it's hard to understand what I'm saying," she explained, "but God truly made families for a reason. He wanted us to grow together and thrive and learn to love and forgive each other. I missed doing that with my brother. I never stopped wondering about him, thinking about him and praying for him. The detective did a great job in locating him. He kept hitting dead ends and finally got a lead. It took nearly a year for him to find him. My sister and I saved our own money for the research and investigation. It was part of the inheritance from our father. He had it put aside for our weddings, but we both agreed that we'd rather have our brother than a wedding. So we authorized the investigator to spend up to a certain amount in his search, plus a ticket home if our brother is found."

Cedric stood up and extended his hand. "Briana, I pray that your brother comes home. I understand what it feels like when part of your family is missing. We hope to see you on Christmas," he said as they both walked away from the table and out to their cars.

Chapter Forty-four

BONNIE BUTLER SMILED as she prepared for landing. She felt like doing a traditional countdown because in just seconds she would be landing in the United States. It had been at least three years since she had been in her native country. It felt good. Christmas was only a few days away. Although she knew she wouldn't spend it with her own family, she was happy for the invitation to visit Charlie's mom. She figured it would be a nice, quiet family holiday.

Although Charlie said he felt well enough to sit in a passenger seat, the rank and file would not have it. So he was transported all the way from Germany on the hospital bed in the military plane. The trip was sure to be interesting, even if it was uneventful, Bonnie Butler believed.

When they got off the plane, an ambulance awaited to transport Charlie to the veterans hospital. The weather was cold and damp, with only a ray of sunshine peeking through the gray clouds. Much care was taken to ensure that Charlie and Bonnie Butler were shielded from the elements.

Charlie was now fully awake and asking questions about the road trip.

The attendant who accompanied the two of them explained that they would be at the hospital in approximately 30 minutes. Charlie closed his eyes and continued to relax. As they neared the hospital, Bonnie Butler spied a noisy commotion as she rode in the ambulance cab.

"What's going on?" Bonnie asked the driver.

"Beats me," the driver answered politely. "Oh," he said, "I think it's their Christmas parade."

BONNIE REACHED DOWN to grab her purse and attaché case. When she raised her head, the crowd opened up and there was a tuba player and a small brass band.

They were now at a full stop, so Bonnie got out of the ambulance. Behind the brass band a sign was stretched between two young people who appeared to be candy stripers. Bonnie threw her head back and laughed when she saw the sign. She hurried to get to Charlie who was being removed from the ambulance wagon.

"Soldier, can you lift your head enough to read the sign?" she teased. Charlie elevated his head and read, 'Welcome home, Charlie, America's hero.' Charlie smiled and looked at Bonnie. "Did you order that?" he asked.

"I had no idea," Bonnie said. "We've been in a foreign land so long, we forgot how much the people we are fighting for really care," she said. A television cameraman and reporter approached Bonnie while the brass band played "I'll Be Home for Christmas."

"Good afternoon, soldier. I'm Dan Russell with WELK TV. We were told if you approve, we could interview our hero," he said.

"I'm sorry," Bonnie said. "No interviews are possible until the soldier receives clearance from our military physician."

"I understand," Mr. Russell said as if he expected that outcome. "Come on, Jack," he said leading the cameraman to a particular spot. "We'll do the stand up over there. Just get some footage of our hero and the band before I do the broadcast," he said.

Bonnie followed the stretcher inside the hospital, stopping to salute and shake hands with various members of the crowd. An army nurse told the attendant to take Charlie to Room 306.

"Major Butler, I'm Nurse Henderson. Welcome back to the states," she said.

"It's good to be home," Bonnie replied.

"I understand you have some paperwork for me," Nurse Henderson said looking anxious. "The quicker we complete everything, including tests, the sooner this soldier can get home to his waiting family," she explained.

167

"Absolutely," Bonnie replied.

"We've already processed a few of the boys from Iraq this week," Nurse Henderson said. "If you would follow me to the office, we can get this party started. It's beginning to look a lot like Christmas," she sang as they went down the hall. "How about some coffee or eggnog?" she offered.

Upstairs in the assigned room for Charlie, a doctor, a food attendant and a nurse were visiting in his room. He had been removed from the stretcher to the hospital bed.

"I'll have the biggest burger you can make," Charlie said. "I'd like an order of applesauce and a Coke," he said looking at the menu. The food attendant took the menu, looked at the doctor and left promptly.

The doctor listened to Charlie's heart and checked his ears.

"Looks like you're doing great, soldier," the doctor said. "I'm afraid that burger will have to wait until I complete a couple of tests and we'll go from there," he said.

When he finished, the nurse took Charlie's blood pressure and checked his temperature. She was documenting her results when Bonnie walked in with a military reporter.

Charlie saluted her from the bed and laughed out loud. "You're the only person I don't mind saluting," he said.

"At ease, soldier," Bonnie replied. "I have two orders of business. One is for you to make an official phone call to your mother, and the second is for you to give some basic unclassified information to this gentleman, Sergeant Andy Pendleton. He's a military reporter for the Army Readiness Command. He wants to do a feature story for the army newsletter's Christmas edition.

"Is it alright if I get a picture of you on the telephone?" Sergeant Pendleton asked. "We held up the newsletter to include your story, so I actually have a deadline of two hours," he said looking at his watch. This edition hits tomorrow. It will be both electronic and printed," he continued.

"Do you still recall your mom's phone number?" Bonnie asked.

"Absolutely, she's had it about 15 years," he said. Bonnie handed the phone to him and moved out the way as he punched in the number and the sergeant snapped a number of pictures.

"Hi, Mom," Charlie said sounding like a frog was in his throat. He covered his eyes with his free hand as he held the phone and pushed back tears at the same time.

Chapter Forty-five

CHRISTMAS DAY

Rachel was so nervous as she lit the candles on the dining table. She turned an ordinary table of four into seating for six. She then added an attractive single candle inside a gold trimmed wreath on the card table. The table cloths were green and gold, respectively. She used the fancy set of dishes that Charlie had shipped her from overseas several years ago. She remembered telling him that she would probably never have an occasion to use such a set. She smiled as she considered how wrong she had been. The flatware wasn't real silver, but the pieces matched. She had to purchase glasses at the discount store. She had never had ten unchipped glasses at one time.

She stood back and felt satisfied that her children would be proud. Then she plugged in the lights that trimmed her Blue Spruce Christmas tree. Next she checked on the beautiful ham decorated with pineapple rings and cherries. It was glazed to perfection. She stirred the meatballs in their sweet and sour sauce. This was Charlie's favorite dish ever since he was a young teen. The special Christmas punch was chilling in the refrigerator above the tossed salad and cranberry orange salad. She kept the potatoes and green beans in the oven to keep them warm. Now she would discard the apron and freshen up a little more. Hopefully she would have a moment to herself before the guests arrived.

On the way to her bedroom, Rachel found the special Christmas FM station that she loved to listen to each year. She put the volume on low and began untying her red and green apron from her waist. She was suddenly interrupted by the apartment buzzer just as Bing Crosby sang the classic "Do You Hear What I Hear."

She hurried to release the knot in the apron and went to answer the door. It was Cedric and his hands were full.

"Now I see why you didn't use your key," his mom said opening the door as wide as she could.

"Merry Christmas, Mom," he said, walking towards the tree to place the gifts beneath it.

He placed an arm full of narrow, red and green wrapped packages beneath the tree. They were all the size of a watch box. He then took a look around. "Everything looks so nice," he said. "Can I help you with anything?"

The buzzer rang again before she could answer. "Would you get the door while I touch up my make-up?" Rachel said.

Rachel went into her bedroom and closed the door behind her. She really wanted a moment to herself to give thanks. Her son would soon be home after several years of being away. She was nervous, grateful and excited as she reached for her makeup box.

Cedric opened the door to Melissa, Buster and another woman.

"Merry Christmas!" they yelled simultaneously as they each came through the threshold.

"This is Graciela," Buster said. "My fiancé."

"Just call me Grace," she said as she accepted the open arms of Cedric. He hugged each of them and gave a smile and warm embrace to Melissa, who handed him a dessert that she had made for the occasion.

"What kind of cake is this?" Cedric asked.

"It's a pound cake that I made from Mom's recipe," she said proudly.

"Thanks so much! Please let me take your coats," he offered. "Mom will be out in a moment."

RACHEL MADE HER GRAND ENTRANCE from the bedroom while Cedric took the coats into the spare room. He and Charlie once shared bunk beds in the space. While hanging the coats in the spare closet, he looked around and saw that his mom had put out old pictures of him and his brother. He nearly got caught up in reminiscing, but a loud commotion came from the living room area. He hurried back just in time to see Charlie in a bear hug of an embrace with his mom. Cedric wanted to cry but held back the tears to join the hug for a truly family embrace.

Rachel tried to talk, but her words were tangled because her heart was full. A female soldier stood by in uniform and handed a handkerchief to Charlie. "Everyone," Charlie said loudly, "this is Bonnie Butler."

Grace got up from the couch and gave Bonnie a Christmas hug. "I'm Grace, Buster's friend," she said. "Why don't I take your coat?"

Grace began taking Bonnie's coat when the buzzer again rang.

"I'll get it, Mom," Cedric said, since Rachel was still hugging and kissing her son.

Cedric opened the door to find two young ladies. "Merry Christmas!" he said warmly. "Please come in," he said. "Hey everybody, these are Mr. Stan's daughters, Briana and …"

"Jackie," the other young lady answered. Rachel turned her attention toward the young ladies and gave them a hug as well.

"I'm turning into an awful host," Rachel said, wiping her eyes. "I am truly happy to see each of you, and now it's time to eat dinner," she said. "The powder room is down the hall on your right and we have two tables for dining," she said almost apologizing. Fortunately, they both fit in my oversized dining room, so hopefully we should all be able to hear one another.

"Can I help you serve, Aunt Rachel?" Melissa asked.

Rachel put both hands to her face to hold back tears. "It's so nice to be called that again," she said. "Absolutely, please do."

THE CONVERSATION WAS THRILLING, listening to Charlie's exploits and Buster's rescues and Rachel telling of her new experience as a Christian. Grace told of her recent airplane drama, Bonnie told of her conversion, Melissa spoke of her freedom from addiction and unbelievable court case dismissal. Then the girls, Briana and Jackie, told of what they remembered of their father.

"Which reminds me," Cedric said, "we have the tickets for you." Melissa pulled a laminated ticket from her purse and handed it to Cedric who then gave it to Briana.

"Wow!" Charlie said suddenly.

"Is something wrong?" Rachel asked.

"No," he said, "but listening to Grace talk about her near plane crash experience just brought to mind something. Oh my God!"

"Charlie, are you having flashbacks?" Bonnie asked in almost an official capacity.

"Last night I dreamed that before the bomb went off, I dropped the grenade when I fell. There was this figure, this tall man that said, 'You dropped something!' That was the last thing I remembered. I just heard that three times tonight. Grace, you mentioned the tall man behind your seat on the plane who handed the ticket to the man you were witnessing to on the plane. Buster, you said a tall man got in front of you on the bridge and prevented you from being in the pile up. Mr. Stan whispered in my ear twenty years ago something that I never told anyone. I was too traumatized to remember it until now. He said, there's an angel behind you. I remember walking away and Daddy Long Legs made me pick up my ticket that I had thrown to the ground. He said the same words. 'You dropped something.' I think Daddy Long Legs was an angel."

"I've got goose bumps," Jackie said. Everyone began talking at the same time when the buzzer rang again. Only a few heard it, including Cedric who went to answer it.

Cedric came around the corner to the dining room and called out Charlie's name. Everyone got quiet.

"Charlie, did you tell the reporter about the ticket exchange when you did your interview?" he asked.

"Well, yes, I may have mentioned it, because Mom told me about it on the phone. I think I said it was off the record," Charlie explained.

173

"The reporter must have missed that part," Cedric said. "He talked about the homecoming and the ticket exchange, and that information has gone out in the newsletter. Anyway, there's a young man here who said he read it and got your address from someone at the hospital. He says it was his father who was killed that day in the accident."

"It's our brother!" Briana said jumping up with Jackie. They both ran to the door and were met by Lieutenant Hutson. Everyone followed and stared. Briana and Jackie stopped suddenly in their tracks.

"Hutson?" Charlie exclaimed. "Lieutenant Hutson!" He gave him a great, big hug. Was Mr. Stan your father?" he asked.

"Who?" Lieutenant Hutson responded.

"I thought Cedric said your father was killed in the accident," Charlie said.

"He was. My father had a heart attack while driving. He was the one who hit the other truck that day," he explained.

There was complete silence. Everyone stared at each other for a moment's eternity. Cedric went forward and broke the silence.

"Please have a seat, Lieutenant Hutson," Cedric said. "I want you to accept my sincerest apology. For years we were so focused on Mr. Stan that we never stopped to consider that someone else lost their loved one on that day. It's so ironic or miraculous that both you and Charlie served in the same outfit. This night was about returning the tickets to the ones they were originally designed for. But we've got more than we ever imagined."

Charlie looked at Bonnie. "Bonnie, did you happen to bring the ticket I asked you to keep?"

"I've got it right here," Bonnie said.

"I'd like to give my ticket to Lieutenant Hutson," he said. "He's the one who found me and recovered my sick body in the mountains of Iraq." Everyone gasped with joy and shock. "I think Mr. Stan would approve," Charlie said.

174

The buzzer rang again, and Cedric answered.

"I'm looking for Briana," a voice said. "She left instructions to meet her at this address if I made it to town."

"Please come in," Cedric said, closing the door behind him.

CEDRIC STEPPED OUT OF THE WAY and a tall, young man stood in front of his sisters for the first time in nearly 20 years. The sisters slowly made their way to the door and fell on the chest of their brother. Jackie's twin and Briana's little brother. He moved into the apartment and greeted everyone with Merry Christmas through tear-stained eyes as he loved on his long lost loved ones.

Grace stepped out from behind the others and said, "Mark?"

The young man looked down and said, "Grace? What are you doing here?" Everyone's expressions and heads went back and forth between Grace and Mark as if they were watching a tennis match.

Almost in a state of disbelief, Grace explained her familiarity with him. "Mark is the person who was seated next to me on the plane that nearly went down. Buster, I wasn't sure how to tell you that I told him he could keep my ticket."

"Oh my God," Rachel said. "The angel or Daddy Long Legs was sitting behind you on the plane."

Mark looked puzzled. "We will fill you in on all the details, Mark," Grace said. "But for now it appears that the love of God has been pursuing you for a long time. You were never off God's radar, Mark. He did hear you when you called on him many years ago. This night was meant to be, and God orchestrated the whole thing. God is the only one who can make something good come out of pain and make a wonderful ending to a life of wandering and suffering. Welcome home, Mark. You're right where God wants you," Grace said feeling she was standing in a miracle moment.

She gave him a hug too, although his sisters never let him go. They were speechless and lost in the glory of peace on earth. At least it was for them, after a lifetime of incompleteness. They finally felt whole.

"Let's give this family a moment to get reacquainted," Cedric said, turning away from a scene more powerful than a Norman Rockwell painting. He turned his attention to the Christmas tree and retrieved the beautifully wrapped narrow boxes he had placed there earlier. He began passing them out to everyone in the room.

"They're all the same," he said. "I just wanted to capture this special day that I had no idea would turn out so incredibly wonderful," he said. "Charlie, why don't you open yours first because we wouldn't be gathered together here on this beautiful Christmas if God hadn't sent you home to us."

Charlie smiled and grabbed Bonnie's hand and brought her closer to him as he removed the gold paper from the white box and found inside three leather engraved bookmarks. He read aloud the gold etching on the front, This is Your Ticket to Heaven. He continued reading the scripture placed beneath the title.

"For God so loved the world that he gave his only begotten son, that whosoever believeth in Him should not perish but have everlasting life." John 3:16

"You may want to keep one as a keepsake," Cedric advised, "but for heaven's sake, be sure to give the other two away."

"This is the most wonderful Christmas ever," Charlie said looking up. It was just in time. The radio was playing the ending to the song "O Come Let Us Adore Him Christ the Lord."

– The End –

About the Author

SANDRA THOMPSON WILLIAMS is a native of Saint Louis, Missouri. She received her Bachelor's degree in communication from Saint Louis University and worked more than 15 years in public relations for educational institutions. She currently works for Saint Louis County Library.

A praise and worship leader at her local church, Sandra enjoys music that reaches the heart of the Father. In 2012, she released her first CD Songs of Deliverance. A licensed missionary through her local assembly, she is also a dedicated Sunday school teacher.

Sandra is the author of "Eating the Fruit of Lies" and "The Invocation," both novels; and "Even Better Than Aunt Harvey's Greens," a devotional, and co-author of "Ye Shall Receive Power: The Spiritual Life of Vera Boykin," a biography. She has also authored "Seven Miracles of Prevailing Praise." In addition to writing, Sandra enjoys singing, traveling, and discovering hidden truths in the Bible.

She resides in the St. Louis Metropolitan area.

26813849R00109

Made in the USA
Columbia, SC
19 September 2018